Y0-ARX-009

OUR EARTH

OUR EARTH

by

GERTRUDE WHIPPLE

SUPERVISOR OF READING, DETROIT PUBLIC SCHOOLS AND
ASSOCIATE PROFESSOR OF EDUCATION, WAYNE UNIVERSITY

and

PRESTON E. JAMES

PROFESSOR OF GEOGRAPHY, SYRACUSE UNIVERSITY

Cartography by

ARTHUR H. ROBINSON

ASSISTANT PROFESSOR OF GEOGRAPHY,
UNIVERSITY OF WISCONSIN

THE MACMILLAN COMPANY *NEW YORK*

1948

PRINTED IN THE UNITED STATES OF AMERICA

Published March, 1947.
Reprinted October, 1947, July, 1948.

ACKNOWLEDGMENTS

THIS BOOK would have been impossible in its present form had it not been for the resourcefulness and imagination of the photographer responsible for most of the kodachromes, namely Konstantin J. Kostich.

Acknowledgment is made of the services of Eugene Kingman in the preparation of the art work for the maps used in this book.

The authors also wish to acknowledge with gratitude the assistance of Mrs. Dorothy Cooper of the Detroit Public Schools in assembling certain subject matter incorporated in the chapters of this book.

FOR THE BOYS AND GIRLS

We live on the earth. If we were high up in the sky, we could look down upon the earth. Then we should see that it looks like a huge ball. It is so very huge that you can see only a tiny part of it at a time. For this reason the earth looks flat to us.

Because the earth is round like a ball, it is called a sphere, or a globe. It is a very, very large sphere.

The earth is made of land and water. People live on the land. Some people have farms to raise food. Some people raise animals to get meat. These animals eat grass or plants that grow on the land. Men grow food for these animals to eat.

Much of the earth is covered with water. There are small ponds, many streams, and great seas. Fish live in the water. Men catch the fish for food.

From streams on the earth people get water to drink. They get water in other ways too. Sometimes they dig deep down into the earth until they reach water. Everyone needs water. If you could not get water to drink, you would soon die.

Some of our clothes are made from parts of plants. These plants grow on the earth. Some clothes are made from the hair or the skin of animals which live on the earth.

Our houses are built partly of wood. Wood comes from trees which grow on the earth. Rock is also used in building houses. Some rock is found on top of the ground, and some is dug from within the earth. The rock has to be cut into pieces of the right size.

So everything we have comes from the earth, from either the land or the water. Without the earth we would have no food and no houses, and we could not make clothes.

The stories in this book tell about the earth. They tell how people use the land to make a living. They tell about the water on the earth and the air around it.

When you turn the next page, you will see a picture of the earth. Of course, you can see only half of it at a time. It is the half on which we live. In the picture all the land is colored light brown. Though the land looks small in the picture, it is really very, very large. It is so large that nobody has ever seen all of it. In the picture the water is blue.

On the earth is a point named the north pole. When you go toward this pole from any part of the world, you are going north. If you could stand at the north pole, the north star would be right up over your head.

Just at noon turn your back to the sun. You will then be looking toward the north pole. Your back will be toward the south pole. The direction south means toward the south pole. The direction in which the sun rises is east. The direction in which it sets is west.

Very far north in the picture is the north pole. It is the farthest north that we can go on our earth. The south pole is farther south than any other point on our earth.

Exactly halfway between the poles a make-believe line goes around the earth. This line is called the equator. You can see it in the picture.

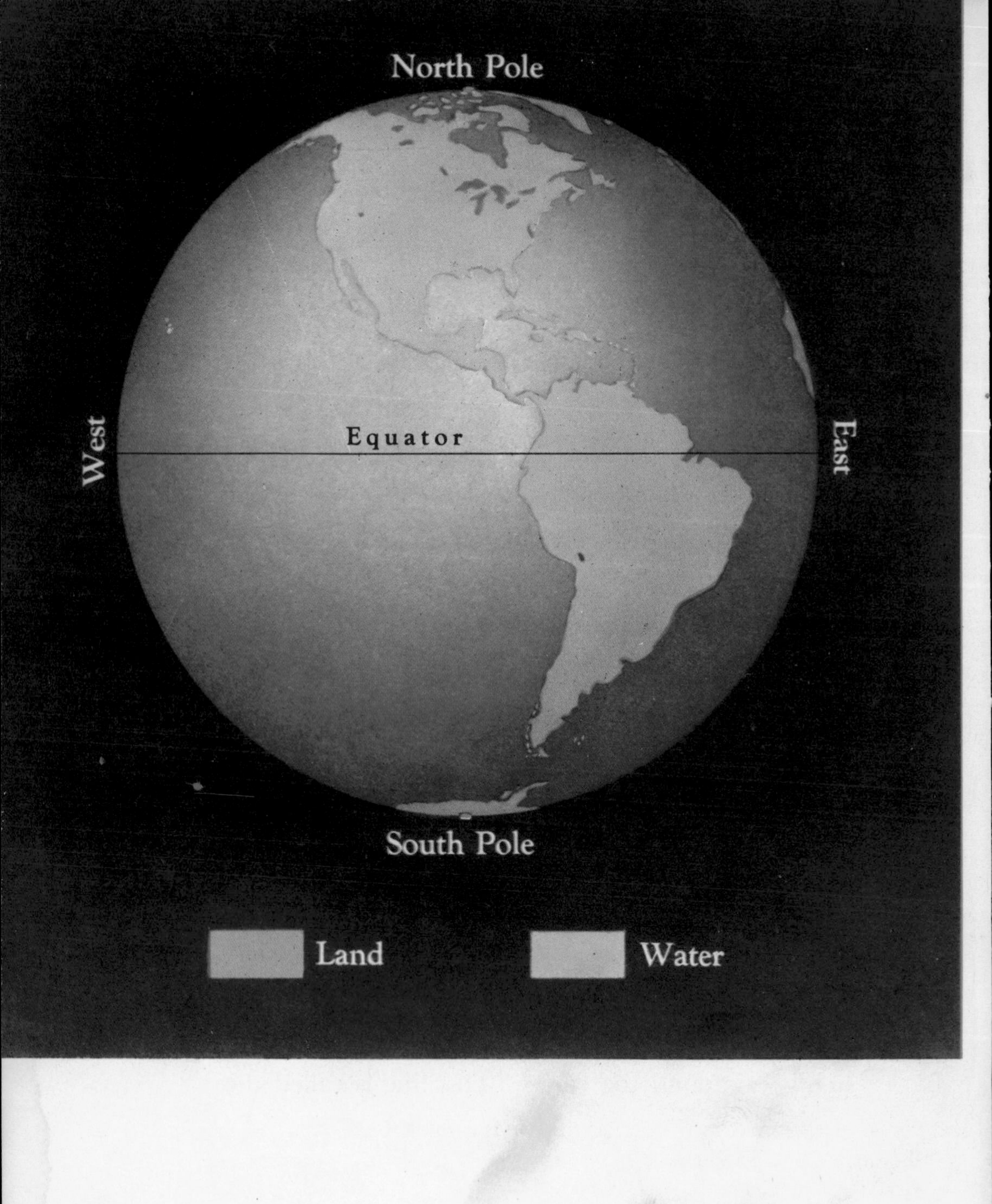
North Pole
West
Equator
East
South Pole
Land
Water

TABLE OF CONTENTS

Mountain Stories

THE SHEEP HERDER AND HIS DOGS

Look at the first picture. In the middle of it you see animals walking. They are sheep. They have come up among very high hills, called mountains, to eat grass. You know that little sheep are called lambs.

The man who takes care of the sheep is called the herder. His name is John Ward. While the sheep are eating grass, he sits on the stump of a tree and watches them.

How many dogs does the herder have? He raised his dogs from the time when they were puppies. The dog with the white neck is Shep. The other is Spot. They have long, rough hair.

John Ward has trained his dogs to work with him. What work do you think they can do?

The herder is all alone in the mountains. He is far away from his wife and children. But he likes to take care of the sheep and to see that

they have good grass to eat. He likes his dogs, too. Often he talks to them almost as if they were people.

See the flock of sheep. How many sheep can you count easily in this picture? In some flocks there are more than two thousand sheep.

Most of the sheep are eating grass, or grazing. John Ward watches while they graze. When he sees a lamb getting too far away from the flock, he calls to Spot and waves his hand. Spot circles around the lamb and gently brings it back. The herder keeps watch while Spot works.

This flock is made up of ewes, or mother sheep, and their lambs. Most of the ewes have one or two lambs. The herder hopes that his lambs will grow fat on the mountain grass.

While the herder is in the mountains, he camps in a little hut. You can see that it is made of thin logs loosely put together. It can be moved easily when the sheep go to a new place to graze. A place where animals graze is called a pasture.

Why do you think John and Shep left the flock and walked over to the hut?

The herder cannot leave his flock of sheep and go down the mountains to get food. He and his dogs have to stay with the sheep all day and all night. If he left the sheep, wild animals might carry off the lambs.

Another man is hired to bring food to the herder and his dogs. His name is Jim Brown. He is called the camp tender. In the picture you can see him climbing the mountain to reach the pasture. He has two animals following him. They are mules. Mules look much like horses but have longer ears. Men use mules on steep paths. Mules do not slip on a steep path, and they can carry heavy loads.

Jim Brown and his mules travel slowly up the steep sides of the mountain. In some places the path goes straight up a gentle slope without turning to either side. In other places the slope is very steep. Then Jim turns to one side and leads the mules up an easy slope for a while.

The camp tender looks down and sees a deep valley where a stream has cut through. It dashes over the rocks. Trees and bushes grow on the steep sides of the valley.

Soon Jim Brown hears a cry, "Baa, baa." He knows he is coming close to the pasture where a flock of sheep are grazing. The lambs call to their mothers. The ewes call back to their lambs.

Soon the herder sees Jim Brown and his mules. How pleased he is to see his good friend from the valley! He asks about his family, and the camp tender tells him they are all well and happy. Jim Brown has brought letters for the herder.

John Ward is glad to get the bacon, the eggs, and the other foods which Jim has brought. The camp tender also has food for the dogs, Spot and Shep.

But Jim Brown cannot stay and talk. He has to take food to other herders in the mountains. He says good-bye and leaves with his mules.

Then John Ward walks slowly along after the sheep as they graze. He reads a letter which the camp tender brought.

The sheep move slowly, eating the grass. They cut the grass off close to the roots because a sheep has a split lip. You can see the split lip in the picture. If the sheep grazed too long in one place,

the grass would not grow there again. John and his dogs will tend the flock in the mountains all summer.

GRAZING IN THE MOUNTAINS

Early the next morning the sheep scatter out and begin to graze. John Ward cooks his breakfast. He makes coffee and cooks bacon and eggs.

Spot and Shep want a good meal too. They know that their master will feed them soon.

After breakfast the herder puts his pans and dishes away. He folds up his blankets. As he works, he looks far off. He can see snow on the top of the highest mountains. The snow does not melt even in summer because the tops of these mountains never get warm. Grass and flowers are growing in the valleys below. But the mountaintop is so far above the valley that it is cold almost all the time.

The sheep graze until the middle of the day. Then they drink at a clear mountain stream. They put their mouths down into the stream and drink the cool water. Some of them move into the shade of the trees and rest.

In the afternoon the camp tender comes back to move the camp to a new pasture. He takes down the hut and fastens the logs to his mules. He goes ahead to make a new camp for the herder.

Then the herder whistles to his dogs. They circle around the sheep and turn them toward the new pasture. The sheep move slowly along, grazing as they go.

By evening John Ward and his flock reach the new pasture. He finds a place where rocks shut in the sheep. It will be easy here to keep the sheep together.

When night comes, the sheep crowd together and sleep. The herder sleeps too, for it is quiet and dark in the mountains. Hardly anybody lives there.

In the night the dogs hear a noise among the sheep. They bark and wake their master. John Ward grabs the rifle beside his bed and goes out to see what is wrong. Spot dashes off to one side and barks and barks. Soon he comes back waving his tail as if to say that he drove away the enemy. When the herder is sure that all is quiet, he goes back to bed.

All summer long John will keep moving his sheep to new pastures. He cannot let them stay long in one place. The grass must have time to grow after the sheep have grazed.

These forest pastures belong to all of us together. No flock may graze on a pasture long enough to hurt the grass. Our whole country owns this forest.

A man who works for our country takes care of the forest. He is called a forest ranger. Sometimes he comes to see that a herder and his sheep do not stay too long in one place.

He tells the herder about plants that might poison the sheep. John Ward watches for these plants and turns his flock away from them. The ranger knows where the streams are and where the flock can find a safe place to stay at night. The ranger likes dogs. He always pats Shep and Spot and plays with them.

RETURNING TO THE VALLEY

One morning John Ward looks over his flock to see how fat the sheep are. When he came to the mountains, his lambs were small. Now most of them have grown large and round and fat.

But summer is coming to an end. Soon it will be cold in the mountains. Sometimes the snow is deep in these mountains early in September. Then the sheep would not find anything to eat. The mountaintops are so high above the valley that they get very cold. Then John and his sheep start down to a lower pasture. Each day the dogs guide the sheep toward the lower mountains. The valley where they stay in winter is many miles away.

Spot and Shep watch the sheep to see that they do not wander away and get lost. Their master wants to take the flock back home without losing any of the sheep.

See the flock in the pasture. There is another man besides John Ward in the picture. He is a forest ranger. He watches the herder and the dogs gather the sheep.

The sheep graze as they go down toward the lower slopes of the mountains. They are thirsty. They will hurry until they reach a stream. If there is no water on the way, the sheep can go a day or two without water.

John does not like to let his sheep wait long for a drink. But he knows that their green food has water in it.

It gets warmer as the sheep travel toward the valley. It is warmer down in the valley than up in the mountains.

After several days the herder and his flock reach the valley. The land is not rough and steep as it was in the mountains. Now John can ride the mule which Jim Brown brought on his last trip.

Just a little way ahead is a pond. See the sheep hurrying to the side of the pond to drink. John will stop his mule at the edge to give him a drink.

The herder goes a long way without meeting anyone. After he has ridden down out of the mountains, he and his dogs and the sheep travel over land where little but grass and small bushes grows. There are hardly any trees. It will take several days to reach the place where the owner of the sheep lives.

John Ward lives on a very large farm in winter. This farm is used just to raise sheep. The owner of this farm does not raise fruit or grain or any other animals to sell. A big farm on which sheep are raised is called a sheep ranch.

When John reaches the ranch, Spot and Shep help him put the flock in the pasture. The owner of the ranch comes out to meet the herder. The dogs jump up on Mr. Dodd, the owner. They are glad to see an old friend. The herder is glad to get home to his family.

Mr. Dodd will sell some of the lambs for meat. Perhaps you have eaten lamb. The meat of a full-grown sheep is called mutton.

The owner pays John for taking care of the sheep. The herder has worked on this ranch for many years.

When the sheep were in the mountains, John did not have to give them feed. They ate the grass which grew there. But there is not enough grass on the ranch to feed the sheep.

During the winter John will give them feed. Also the sheep will graze on the winter pastures. They will get some of their water by eating snow.

How do you think the sheep will keep warm in the cold winter? Their hair, or wool, grows long and thick. It keeps them warm. See their thick curly coats in the picture.

In the spring many little new lambs will be born. John Ward will be very busy then looking after the ewes and their lambs.

When it gets warm, the sheep will be too hot. Mr. Dodd will have the wool cut off the sheep. See whether you can find out how a man cuts off the wool. We say that he shears the sheep.

All the wool cut from a sheep is called a fleece. The owner of the ranch will sell the fleeces. They will be used to make wool cloth.

After Mr. Dodd has sheared the sheep, he always sees that his sheep are clean. He makes them go down into a narrow pool of water and swim to the end of the pool. He has put something in the water to kill the bugs, or insects, that may be on the sheep. John Ward takes a long stick and pushes each sheep's head under the water at least twice. He wants the water to reach the sheep's eyes and ears. When the herder makes the sheep go through this water, we say he is dipping the sheep. See whether you can learn more about dipping sheep.

After the sheep have been sheared and dipped, they are ready to go to the mountains again. They will stay there all summer with the herder and his dogs to take care of them and find good pastures for them.

In some parts of our country sheep do not go to the mountains in summer. Their owner finds pasture for them on hills or even low mountains on his own ranch. In other parts sheep stay on small farms.

These small flocks can be cared for by the owner while he lives at home. He does not have to go away for the summer. He does not have to live in a hut and have a camp tender bring his food.

But the greater part of our wool and mutton comes from the large flocks of sheep like the one which you have read about.

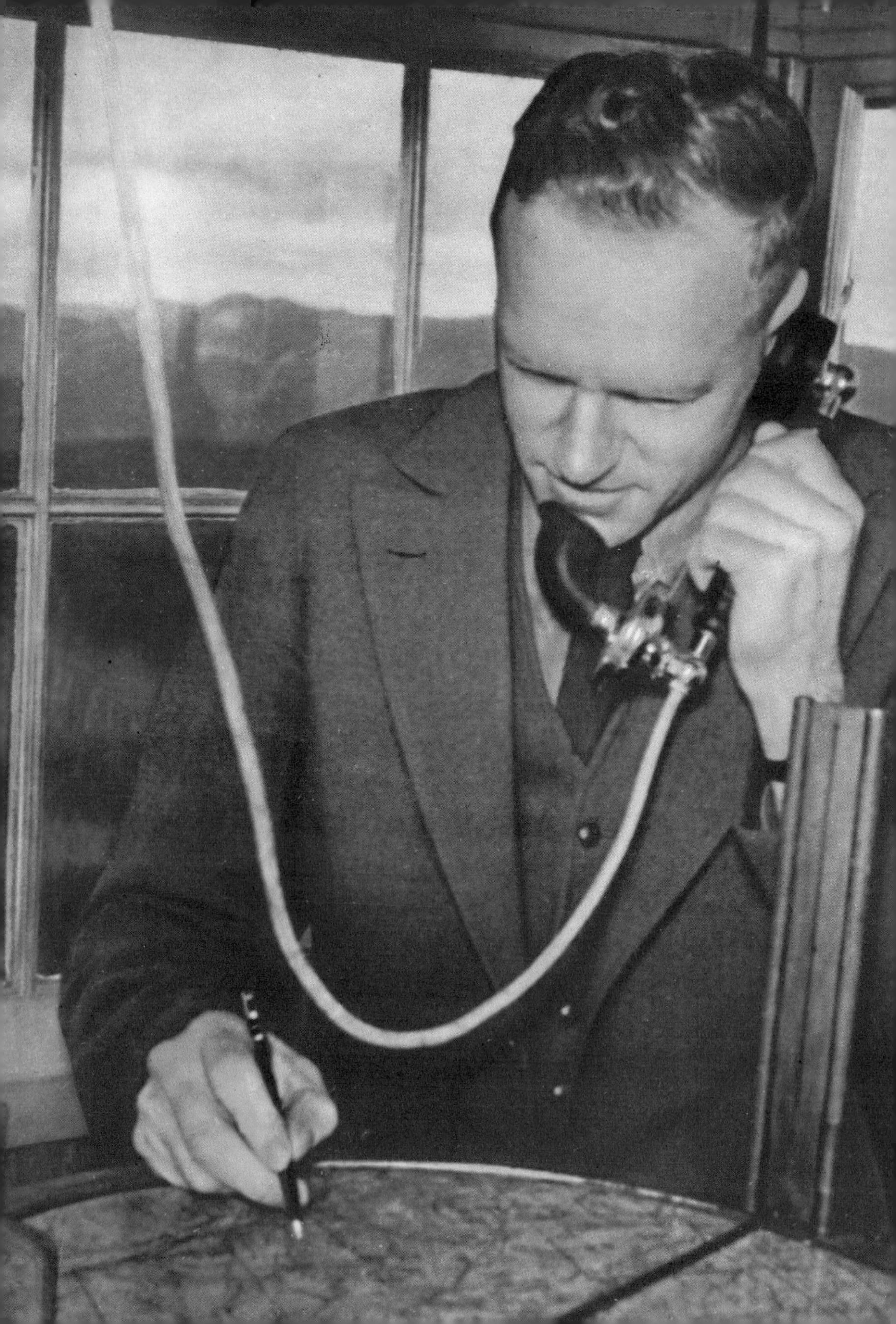

IN THE LOOKOUT TOWER

Sam Tyler is another forest ranger. He lives in a lookout tower on top of a mountain. Trees grow to the top of this mountain. Mr. Tyler watches for fires in the forest. From his tower he looks out over all the mountain slopes around him.

One day Sam Tyler sees smoke rising from the side of a big mountain. He watches and sees that the fire is getting bigger. He knows that the fire is burning on the slope of the mountain named Old Baldy.

Quickly the ranger looks at the big sheet of paper spread out on the table before him. This paper has a picture on it which shows how the forest looks from an airplane up in the air. There are long curvy lines which show the streams and other straighter lines which mark the roads. Other marks show where each mountain is.

Mr. Tyler finds Old Baldy on the picture, or map, to see where the fire is. He knows that the grass and leaves in the forest are very dry. They will catch fire easily. Then the fire will spread. He does not want the fire to burn up the trees or to harm the animals and birds that live on the slopes of Old Baldy.

He reaches for his telephone. Just below Old Baldy is a little town where a fire chief lives. Sam telephones to Chief Stone and tells him about the fire.

Chief Stone sends a man to see how big the fire is. This man is named Jim. Jim has long legs and can climb the steep slopes very fast. He takes a small radio with him.

The fire is close enough for Jim to go on foot. If he should go on a horse or in an automobile, he would have to go a longer way round, because that is the way the road goes.

When Jim reaches the fire, he finds that it is not big. But it is getting bigger. A fallen tree is burning. The flames are jumping up in the air and catching the branches of other trees. Jim can hear the noise of snapping twigs. Leaves

are burning on the ground. The smoke gets into Jim's eyes.

Then Jim begins to talk into his small radio. It is not like the ones which you have seen, for, when Jim asks Chief Stone a question, the chief can answer him. It is like talking over a telephone. Jim tells the chief to send ten or twelve men to fight the fire. He asks that the men hurry, for the fire is spreading fast.

Chief Stone calls for his fire fighters, and they come running. He always has trucks and tools ready for fighting fires. He keeps them in the little town near the foot of Old Baldy.

The men who are to fight the fire put axes and shovels and other tools into one of the trucks. They will use these tools to fight the fire. Then the fire fighters get into the other truck and start out on a road. They are going to the fire on the slope of Old Baldy.

See the fire fighters riding in their truck along the forest road. They drive fast until the road gets steep. They cannot see where the fire is, for it is higher up on the mountain. But they know where to go. The ranger has telephoned,

and the fire chief has shown them the place on his map.

The forest ranger in his lookout tower watches the smoke while the men are fighting the fire. He wonders whether they can keep it from spreading. He does not want Old Baldy to have bare slopes. Then animals cannot graze on Old Baldy.

Mr. Tyler has no neighbors and lives a lonely life. He must stay in the tower all the time when twigs and leaves are dry enough to burn. But he knows it is important to watch for smoke and to send word to the fire chiefs whenever he sees smoke.

FIGHTING A FOREST FIRE

As the men go to the fire in their trucks, the wind begins to blow. A strong wind will blow the flames quickly from tree to tree. The fire will travel fast in the forest. The men know that they must hurry.

Soon the trucks stop. They cannot go any closer to the fire. The men take their tools and start up a steep path as fast as they can go.

As they come near to the fire, they smell the smoke. Then they see the fire. It is running along the ground burning dry leaves, twigs, grass, and bushes. It is killing small trees and hurting large trees.

One of the men looks down and sees a little forest animal running into a hole in the ground. The animal knows he is in danger and wants to get away from the fire. He will live on the food which he has hidden in the ground.

Some of the men begin making a bare path. They pull up bushes and throw them to one side of the path. They dig up the ground and put earth on top of the weeds and grass. Other men begin cutting down the dead trees which are near the fire. They do this work with their axes. Then they carry the trees to one side of the path. The fire cannot reach them. A dead tree will catch fire more quickly than a live tree. Do you know why?

Do you see the dead trees which the men cut down? Some dead trees are left standing. The men cut down only those which would catch fire easily.

The fire fighters try to make a bare place around the fire. The fire can burn up to this place. But it must stop there unless the wind blows it across. There is nothing to burn in a bare place. Bare places in the path of a forest fire help to keep it from spreading.

A few of the men go close to the fire. They dig earth and throw it on the flames. Then the fire cannot get air. A fire cannot burn without air. Then this fire has to go out. While the men are throwing dirt on the fire, a tree close to them crashes to the ground. Sparks fall on them. They are afraid that their clothes will catch on fire. They grab their hats and beat at their clothes to shake off the sparks. They have to watch where they walk to keep from stepping on hot coals.

Look at this fire fighter at work. What is he doing to help put out the fire? Why is there so much smoke in the forest? How do you think this fire fighter feels?

As the fire fighters work, they get hot and thirsty. There is no stream of water on Old Baldy where they can get a drink. But they know that the fire chief will send them water.

See the man bringing water for the fire fighters to drink. The water is in cans. The cans are fastened on the backs of mules. Soon the fire fighters see the mules coming. They begin shouting for joy. The water cans are taken down from the backs of the mules and handed from man to man. Each one takes a drink of water and goes back to work.

The men work hard to put out the fire. A fire sometimes burns off all the trees and grass on a mountain. When a slope is bare, rain water runs quickly down the slope. It carries away some of the earth and does not sink into the ground. New trees will not grow quickly on a bare slope. There is not enough earth, or soil, for them to grow in.

How glad the men are when they see the last flames go out! The part of the forest which has been burned looks very different now. Many tree trunks are black, and the leaves are gone. Some trees have fallen down. Some are still smoking. The ground is covered with ashes. The grass and bushes are gone. It will take many years for the trees to grow again.

After the fire is out, most of the fire fighters pick up their axes and shovels. They walk down to the trucks and drive back to town. But two or three stay and walk about in the forest. The wind has gone down, but some fallen trees are still smoking. The fire might begin burning again. So these men will wait until there are no more glowing coals to be fanned into a flame. Then they will walk back to town.

This is the way some forests look after a fire. What do you see in the picture? Was the fire in this forest a large or a small one? How do you know?

Sometimes a fire burns and burns before the fire fighters can reach it. It may be too big to be put out. Then the men try to keep the fire from spreading.

How do fires start in a forest? This is one way. People go into the mountains for a good time. They build a little campfire on which to cook their lunch. But when they start home, they forget to put out the fire. Perhaps a strong wind arises and blows sparks into a bunch of dead grass or into a pile of dried leaves. Then they take fire.

Good campers never build a fire against a tree trunk, for the bark, or rough outside covering, will catch on fire. They build their fire on a bare spot of ground, or they clear away the grass or brush before they start the fire. When they leave, they make sure the fire is out. If they are near a stream, they pour water on the fire. If they do not have water, they shovel dirt over the fire until every spark is out.

Sometimes, too, smokers carelessly start fires without wishing to do so. Tell how this happens. People should help protect our forests from fires.

WINTER FUN IN THE MOUNTAINS

Today John Dodd and his father are going to the mountains for a holiday. They are driving there in an automobile. The snow has been cleared off the road. But in some places beside the road it is almost as high as the top of the car.

Soon the little boy and his father come to a valley between two mountain slopes. John wants to skate and slide. The ice on the little pond in the valley is thick. Mr. Dodd knows that the little boy will be safe skating there.

While John puts on his skating shoes, his father watches the boys and girls skating around on the smooth ice. Soon John is skating and shouting with the other children.

Then Mr. Dodd fastens on his skis. Do you see them? He takes a pole in each hand. He

pushes himself along and then begins climbing up the steep slopes. He comes down very fast with the wind whistling in his ears.

Mr. Dodd looks to see that John is having a good time. Then Mr. Dodd starts back up the slope. By putting the long skis down sideways and pushing with the poles, he goes back up the steep slope again.

This time he chooses a slope with pine trees on it. He has to twist about among the trees on his fast slide downhill. He uses the poles to help him turn when he comes to the trees.

Some of the people on skis do not climb up the steep slopes. They like to slide along on the ground in the valley. It is easier to keep from falling if the slopes are gentle. When these people can ski well enough, they will go to the higher slopes on the mountainside.

When John gets tired of skating, he takes off his skating shoes and puts on his other shoes. He climbs up a hill above the pond and sits down on the icy slope. Then he slides down the slope. At the bottom he tumbles into the soft snow. Falling is part of the fun.

In the picture you can see a house where the people can rest and get warm. When the sun shines bright, many of the people stay outside and talk. If they have done much skating or skiing, they have kept warm because they have been moving about.

Soon John and his father will take their skates and skis to the automobile and start home. It gets dark early in winter, and they want to reach home before night. They have had a good time in the snow. But they are tired and hungry now.

WHAT IS A MOUNTAIN?

Do you now understand what a mountain is? Have you ever stood on a mountain? Have you ever seen mountains in the movies? A mountain is like a very high hill. It is so high that you can look down upon even the highest buildings on the land below the mountain. It is so high that you can see a very long way from the top. You can also see the mountain when you are a long way off from it.

See the mountains in the picture. The mountain which is farthest away is higher than the others. Its top is in the clouds. Snow lies on this mountain-top all the year. Some mountains have snow on their tops only in the cold winter.

What does the high mountain in the picture look like? It is a point of land standing up above the rest. High points like this one are called peaks, or mountaintops. If you were in the mountains,

you might see many mountain peaks. They would not all have the same shape as this peak.

Mountains have many different shapes. Some are rounded and do not have a pointed top. Other mountains have very steep slopes. Try to draw a high mountain which would be hard to climb. Try to draw a rounded mountain. You might climb a hill in a few minutes. But it would take you many hours to climb a high mountain. Some mountains are so high and steep that men spend days climbing to the top.

It would get colder and colder as you went up the mountain. Some mountains are so cold at the top that people cannot live there very long without shelter.

When there are many mountains in a row, they are called a range of mountains. The mountain range may be rocky, with few trees growing on the slopes, or it may be covered with trees all the way to the top.

Men have made roads in many of our mountain ranges. But there are still many places in the mountains of our own country where people have never been.

In Hilly Lands

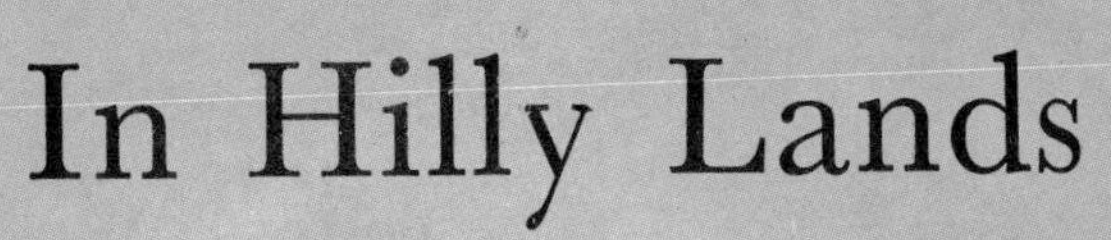

SUGAR-MAKING TIME

Carl Nickerson is going to look at his maple trees. He has many sugar-maple trees growing on his farm. His dog Blackie likes to run along beside him.

Today winter is almost over. But the snow has not yet melted.

Before long Carl comes to a large grove of sugar maples. There are not as many trees in a grove as in a forest. Carl takes care of these trees because he gets maple sap from them. He uses the sap to make maple sugar. It is a very sweet brown sugar. Sometimes he makes maple sirup too.

Carl Nickerson stops and looks at the trees. Blackie runs through the grove, barking. Then he comes back to his master's side. He likes to stop and dig into the snow with his front paws.

Carl sees that some very large branches have fallen during a winter storm. He stoops and picks up these branches. He takes them out of the grove so that they will not be in the way when he drives his horses through the grove.

The trees in the grove are close together, but there are narrow paths between them. When Carl comes to get sap from the trees, he will use these paths. The paths go gently up and down, for the grove is on a hill.

After Carl has cleared away all the larger fallen branches, he and his dog walk slowly back to the house.

The next day Carl goes to the maple grove again. This time he leaves the dog at home. Blackie whines now that his master has left. Sometimes Blackie gets in the way when Mr. Nickerson is working.

See Carl standing by the maple tree. He has cleaned a little place on the side of the tree. He cleaned off the dirt and loose bark with a stiff brush.

He is making a small hole in the tree. He turns a sharp tool around and around in the tree. The

hole is so small that it will fill up again. When a little hole like this is made in the sugar maple tree in the spring, sap comes out. We say the farmer is tapping the tree.

Then Mr. Nickerson drives a strong tube into the hole. It is hollow like the tubes, or straws, which you drink sodas through. But it is larger than the straws and much stronger.

Carl then hangs a bucket on the tube. When the sap comes out through the tube, it will drop into the bucket. Next he taps another tree and hangs a bucket on that tree.

Then he hears Blackie barking and sees the dog running toward him. Blackie does not like to stay at home when his master is away.

How many trees has Mr. Nickerson tapped? He keeps on working, for he wants to tap all the trees in his grove. He has more than two hundred trees. In a few large trees he makes two holes and hangs two buckets on tubes. But usually he makes only one hole in a tree.

The sap drips slowly into the bucket. If the weather is very cold, the sap freezes at night. But frozen sap is good too.

GATHERING MAPLE SAP

Soon all the trees are tapped, and sap is flowing. Then Mr. Nickerson hitches two horses to a sledge. He rides on the sledge. See the big tank to put the sap in. The sledge has runners to go over the snow. Mr. Nickerson is driving to his maple grove.

Blackie likes to ride with his master on the sledge. Sometimes he jumps off and runs ahead of the horses, barking.

The horses pull the sledge down into the valley and up the hill.

When they reach the grove, Mr. Nickerson calls "Whoa." The horses stop. Then Mr. Nickerson goes to one of the trees. He looks down into the bucket and sees that the sap is not frozen today. He tastes it. It is sweet but not as sweet as maple sugar.

Then Carl gets a big bucket off his sledge. This

bucket will hold much more sap than the pail on the tree. Carl takes the pail of sap from the tree and empties the sap into his big bucket. See him emptying the pail. Then he hangs the pail on the tube again. See the pail on the tree. Why is it covered?

Now Carl goes from tree to tree and empties the sap from the pails. When the big bucket is full of sap, he goes back to the sledge. He empties the sap into the big tank and puts the bucket down. Then he says "Giddap" to his horses, calls to Blackie, steps on the sledge, and drives on a little way.

It is such a bright sunny day that Carl enjoys working in his maple grove. He looks up through the bare branches at the blue sky. How glad he is to be out in the woods again after the long, cold winter!

He goes on through the grove gathering maple sap. If you could look into the tank, you would see that it is almost full of sap. The sap will make good maple sugar. When the tank is full, Carl takes up the reins and speaks to his horses. Then they start back over the hills.

AT THE SUGARHOUSE

It is quiet in the grove as Carl Nickerson turns his horses toward a little house called a sugarhouse. Carl drives his horses along the road to the sugarhouse. This is the house where he will make the sap into maple sugar and sirup.

Outside the sugarhouse is a large tank for holding maple sap. From this tank a small pipe runs inside the sugarhouse to the vats, or big pans in which the sap is boiled.

How will Carl empty the tank on his sledge? At the bottom of the tank is a pipe. Another pipe runs along the ground to the receiving tank. See Carl fitting the two pipes together. The sap will run through the pipes down to the big tank. When Mr. Nickerson is ready to boil the sap, he will let it run into the vats.

Carl is a busy man during the maple-sugar season. He must drive through the grove and gather the sap.

He must also make all the sap into sugar or sirup.

When he is ready for this work, he lights the fires under the vats. Then he boils the sap until it is a thick sirup. He knows just how thick the sirup must be to harden into cakes of sugar. Once the fires are lighted, they are kept burning until all the sap in the tank has been made into sirup or sugar.

Carl sells most of the maple sugar and sirup which he makes. Sugaring time comes so early in the spring that he is not busy planting or harvesting crops. This is one kind of work which he can do in early spring to help make a living.

A SUGARING PARTY

At sugaring time the Nickerson children, Tom and Ann, plan to give a maple-sugar party. They invite the children who live on the other farms near by. The party is to be in the sugarhouse after school is out. Blackie hears the children as they come shouting toward the little house. He goes to meet them, barking and wagging his tail.

Inside the sugarhouse Mr. Nickerson has kept the fire burning. Steam is rising from the big vats. As the maple sap boils, Mr. Nickerson watches to see when it is of the right thickness for making sugar.

The children stand and watch the bubbling sap. They have often seen sugar made, but some of the farmers in their part of the country do not have a sugarhouse. They do not have as many trees as Mr. Nickerson. They boil the sap outdoors in a big kettle. They build a fire under the kettle and boil a little sap at a time.

Ann and Tom tell their friends it is time to hunt a patch of clean snow. The children fill plates with snow and go back to the sugarhouse. Mr. Nickerson dips some of the sirup up in a wooden spoon. As drops fall from the spoon, they look like silk threads.

Each child holds out his pan of snow, and Mr. Nickerson pours a spoonful or two of the sirup slowly over the snow. It hardens like candy. The children pick it up and eat it. Later Mr. Nickerson tells them that it is time to leave if they want to get home before dark.

Mr. Nickerson cannot go home until all the sirup boils down just right. Then he puts it into a pan to cool. When it begins to thicken, he stirs it rapidly until it is just right to make sugar. Next he pours the thick sirup into molds, or small pans having the shape in which he wishes the sugar to harden. After the molds are cold, he turns them over. Out come the cakes of maple sugar.

Sometimes Carl does not let the sap boil so long. Before it is thick enough to make into cakes of sugar, he pours it into tin cans. He puts a tight cover on each can. He sells these cans of maple sirup which will keep a long time.

ON A DAIRY FARM

Jane is a little girl just ten years old. She lives on a farm and has a strange pet. Her pet is a large black and white cow named Bess. This morning Jane is helping her father turn the cows into the pasture.

The brown cows which you will see in a later picture are Jerseys. The black and white cows are Holsteins. Jane's father, Mr. Hern, keeps these cows for the milk which they give. He sells the milk.

After Bess has gone through the gate, she stops and waits for Jane to pet her. The little girl reaches over the fence and pats Bess on the head.

This morning Mr. Hern watches the cows as they go into the pasture and begin to graze. What time of the year is it in the picture? Is it spring or summer or fall? If it were winter where Jane lives, there would be snow on the ground.

The cows walk slowly about the pasture eating

grass. They like young grass best. But they eat long, thick grass, too, and even dry grass. They cannot bite off the grass as close to the ground as sheep do because they do not have split lips.

Jane likes to watch the cows too, but she knows she must not run and play in the pasture. She must not excite the cows. Her father says that it is bad to hurry the cows and to make them run. Then they will not give so much milk.

The cows must have plenty of water during the day. They drink from a stream of clear water that winds through the pasture. They must have water to drink in the barn, where they are kept at night.

During the day the sun is warm. Then the cows like to lie down in the shade. If it is not too warm, they lie down in the sun. Do you see any of the cows lying down?

Each cow moves slowly along, biting off the green grass and swallowing it. She does not chew up the grass as she bites it off. The food goes to a stomach where it is made into soft balls, or cuds.

A stomach is the part of the body where the food

goes when it is swallowed. A cow has four stomachs. How many stomachs have you?

After the cow has grazed awhile, she stops to rest. Sometimes she lies down in the shade, and sometimes she stands still to rest. Then she brings a cud back into her mouth and chews it up. After she has chewed it well, she swallows it again.

If one of Mr. Hern's cows does not chew her cud, he knows that she is sick. The cow may have eaten a plant that was not good for her.

Mr. Hern's cows cannot stray into other fields. He has built a fence around the pasture.

The cows stay in the pasture all day. Jane and her father will not have to take care of them till evening. Jane goes back to the house. It is Saturday, and she does not have to go to school. Her mother is making apple butter. Jane stands near the stove and stirs the cooking fruit to keep it from burning.

Mr. Hern is busy at the barn. He has to work hard so that his cows will have plenty to eat. Last spring he planted corn on part of his farm. There are pictures of corn in this book. Can you find them?

While the corn was still green, Mr. Hern cut some of it up for feed. He cut both the ear of the corn and the stem, or stalk. Then he put this feed into a building called a silo. The silo is the round building with the slanting top near the barn. The feed in the silo is called silage. It will keep well because not much air can get into the silo. When winter comes and there is no green grass, Mr. Hern will feed the silage to his cows. Unless a cow has plenty of feed, she will not give much milk.

While his cows are grazing today, Mr. Hern cleans out the stalls, or little rooms, where the

cows sleep and are milked. He must clean the stalls every day. He fills his wagon with manure, which will be good for the soil in the fields. He drives his wagon to the field. Then he spreads the manure over the ground.

His horses pull a plow over the field. The plow cuts into the ground and turns the soil over on top of the manure. In this way Mr. Hern mixes the manure with the soil. Next spring when the farmer plants grain in the field, the grain will grow fast.

In the late afternoon milking time comes. Mr.

Hern opens the pasture gate. Then the cows start back to the barn. They know when it is milking time.

When the cows come in from the pasture, each one goes to her own place in the barn. She knows that she will find grain in her feedbox. There is a pail of fresh clean water for each cow.

When the cow reaches her stall, she puts her head in the feedbox. Then Mr. Hern slides a piece of wood into place at one side of her neck. Now the cow must stay in the stall because of the stanchion, or collar, around her neck.

Jane likes to watch her father milk the cows. He milks them early in the morning and early in the evening.

Mr. Hern brushes each cow and washes her milk bag. He washes his hands and puts on a white coat. He puts a stool down on the right side of the cow and sits on it while he milks. He takes one of the cow's teats in each hand and holds it between his thumb and fingers. Then he presses it against the palm of his hand, pulling gently at the same time. When he has milked two of the teats, he milks the other two teats in the same way.

The farmer makes the little streams of milk go into the clean bucket.

Jane has not learned how to milk, but her father

has promised to teach her. When her hands are stronger, she will be able to milk Bess.

Mr. Hern always keeps his cows and barn very clean. He wants the milk to be clean. The buckets must be washed and scrubbed every time they are used. Mrs. Hern often lets them stand in the sunshine, too.

After milking time, the farmer weighs each cow's milk. He finds out how much milk he gets from each cow. If a cow does not give enough milk, he may give her different food, or he may sell her for meat.

The farmer carries the milk to a little house called the milkhouse. It is near the barn. He puts the cans of warm milk into a trough through which cool water runs. He wants the milk to cool quickly. Then it will keep until next morning when he is ready to take it to market.

On some farms where there are many cows, the milking is done by a machine. Rubber cups are put over the cow's teats, and the milk goes through a pipe into large cans. But many farmers in our land still milk their cows by hand just as Mr. Hern does.

TAKING MILK TO MARKET

Early the next morning Mr. Hern milks his cows again. Then he goes to the milkhouse. He gets the big cans of milk and puts them on his truck. It stands near the big barn. Do you think the can of milk will be heavy? Mr. Hern lifts the can easily, for he is strong. He swings the big cans on his truck and soon has it loaded.

Part of his milk will be made into cheese. This is why Mr. Hern goes every day to take his milk to the cheese factory, or the place where cheese is made.

A good road runs past Mr. Hern's farm. It is easy for him to take his milk to the cheese factory. If the road were rough, it would be hard for him to go to the factory every day. It would take too much time. Then he would not have time enough to clean out the barn. He would not have time enough to grow feed for his cows.

The road to the factory winds around among the hills. The farmer travels down one hill and up another when he takes his milk to the factory.

As he drives along, he meets other farmers. They have taken their milk to the cheese factory and are going to their homes. Mr. Hern calls "Hello, Jim," to a friend. They talk a few minutes about feeding their cows and then go on their way.

See Mr. Hern's truck on the road. How has he fastened the cans so that they will not fall off?

Before long Mr. Hern reaches the factory. It is in a valley where three roads meet. Why do

you think the owner built his cheese factory there?

Other men drive up with milk cans too. About twenty farmers bring their milk to this cheese factory. There are many other factories where other farmers sell their milk. Inside the factory the good, fresh milk is made into cheese.

After Mr. Hern sells his milk, he puts some empty cans into the truck. Then he gets back into his truck and drives home. Next time he will fill these cans with milk and bring them to the factory.

Every day Mr. Hern takes his milk to the factory. In winter when there are deep snows, he will still

go to the factory. The road will be cleared with a machine called a snowplow.

A farmer who keeps cows for milk as Mr. Hern does is called a dairy farmer. Dairy farmers have to work hard in the spring and summer to provide feed for their cows to eat in the winter.

Some dairy farmers do not take their milk to cheese factories. A man in a big truck stops at their farms and picks up the milk cans. The milk is taken to a place in the city where it is put into bottles. Then milkmen take the bottles of milk to homes, stores, and hotels.

HOW CAN YOU TELL A HILL FROM A MOUNTAIN?

Sometimes a part of the land stands up above the other parts. Yet the higher parts are not big enough to be called mountains. Such land is called hilly land. Is a hill as high as a mountain?

Some hills are covered with trees. Some hills are rocky and bare. Some hills are grassy and can be used for pasture land. Some hills can be used to grow food on.

If the sides of a hill are not too steep, men can plow the ground and raise grain or vegetables there. Fruit trees are often planted on the sunny sides of the hills. Have you ever seen fruit trees on a hillside?

Most hills are easy to climb. If there are valleys between the hills, the valleys are not deep and hard to get through. Sometimes you can climb right up the hill and stand on the top.

Stories of the Plains

RAISING CORN

At the beginning of this story are two pictures. The first picture shows Harry Reed plowing a field. The second picture shows another part of Mr. Reed's farm. You can see how flat the land is.

It is a warm spring morning. Mr. Reed is getting his field ready to plant corn. He uses a plow to cut into the soil and loosen it. His plow is pulled by a tractor, which moves on endless-belt tracks and has an engine in it like the engine of an automobile.

Mr. Reed sits in a seat on the tractor as his plow is pulled straight across the field. The plow turns the soil over and throws it to one side.

After the field has been plowed, Mr. Reed fastens a big rake to his tractor. This rake goes over the big lumps of soil and breaks them up. This big rake is called a harrow. Mr. Reed uses the harrow to make the soil in the field flat, or level.

When the field has been made level, Mr. Reed plants yellow grains of corn. He gets up into the seat of the tractor and pulls another machine up and down the field. This machine drops grains of corn into the ground and covers them over with loose soil.

A few days later it rains hard, and the corn gets moist. The grains of corn start to grow. Soon the little plants push their way above the ground.

While the corn is growing higher, weeds are growing in the field. What is a weed? Mr. Reed has worked hard to keep weeds out of his field. But today he looks at his field and sees that more weeds have come up.

Then Mr. Reed calls his son John and tells him that the weeds are growing fast. John says that he will plow the field and kill the weeds.

John hitches another machine to the tractor. This machine has several small plows. John drives the tractor up and down the cornfield. The small plows turn the earth over between the rows of corn, but do not touch the corn plants. The weeds are covered with soil, and they die.

Mr. Reed goes out every few days to see how his

corn is growing. It grows high and is in straight rows. Mr. Reed is glad that spring showers come up almost every day and water his plants. The warm sunshine helps the corn to grow. But the corn grows all night too, for the soil is warm and moist.

The corn grows higher and higher. Every day it is higher than it was the day before. Soon it is too tall for Mr. Reed to plow between the rows. The cornstalk grows stiff and straight.

The farmer and his family take good care of their fields, for corn is a food which they need. They

feed the grain to their farm animals. Mrs. Reed needs corn for the chickens which she raises. She has white hens and roosters. She sells eggs, and the egg money belongs to her.

Mrs. Reed keeps her chickens in a fenced yard, and they have a house to roost in at night. She feeds the chickens every day. Sometimes she puts pieces of corn bread in a trough in the chicken yard. In another trough she keeps clear, cool water. The chickens like corn, green vegetables, and bugs which they find on the grass.

Every afternoon Mrs. Reed takes a basket and goes into the chicken house. Along the walls inside the house there are rows of nests. Each nest has straw in it. Mrs. Reed looks into one of the nests and finds a white egg. She puts the egg into her basket. She goes from nest to nest and soon has her basket full of large, white eggs.

On one part of the farm Mr. Reed keeps pigs. His pigs have short, thick bodies and legs. They have short, curly tails. Their noses are snouts so that they can root in the ground. The half-grown pigs are kept in a yard with a fence around it. A yard in which pigs are kept is called a pigpen. A

few bushes grow in the pigpen. There is a water trough in the pen where the pigs can always get a drink of water. There is a trough where Mr. Reed puts corn for the pigs to eat.

What do you see in this picture? There are two mother pigs, or sows. The young pigs are feeding. Can you count the little pigs which each sow has? The sow talks to the pigs in grunts. The little pigs make sharp, little squeals in answer. My, what a noise they make!

The pigs will grow into big, fat hogs. Then Mr. Reed will sell them for meat. The meat that we get from hogs is called pork. We also get fat from hogs to make lard.

The farmer likes to look at his cornfields every day, for he needs corn to feed his pigs and chickens. Soon he sees that ears of corn are growing on the stalks.

The hot weather and the rains help the plants to grow big. Many of the stalks grow much taller than a man.

The farmer tells his wife that he will have plenty of corn this year. He can feed his pigs and chickens. He can feed his other farm animals too. What other animals do you think Mr. Reed has?

Mrs. Reed keeps a little sign out in front of her house. The sign says "Fresh eggs." People who drive by in their automobiles stop and honk their horns. Then Mrs. Reed comes out and sells some of her eggs. They are packed in boxes which hold a dozen eggs.

Before the corn is ripe, Mr. Reed tells John and Ben to cut some of it. Ben is a man who works every summer for Mr. Reed. The farmer wants to save the corn plants as green feed for his farm animals.

See John and Ben cutting the corn. The man wears a hat to keep the sun out of his eyes. John does not mind the sun. See how sunburned his face and arms are.

Mrs. Reed knows how hot it is out in the cornfield. When John and Ben come to the end of the field near the house, she takes them a pitcher of cool water.

They turn away from the sun and take a big drink. Ben takes off his hat and wipes his forehead. He fans his face with his hat and then goes back to work.

Ben does not cut down all the corn to make silage. He lets most of the corn stand in the field until the ears become dry. It will be ripe then and make good winter feed for the farm animals.

As John goes along a row, he chops the cornstalks off close to the ground. He and Ben have long, sharp corn knives that cut through the stalks at one blow. They toss the cornstalks into a wagon. The horses stand still, switching their tails to brush the flies off their backs. When John or Ben speaks to them, the horses move on till the boys call out "Whoa." Then the horses stop.

Do you see Ben in this picture? What color are the horses? They are strong work horses. What kind of wagon is Ben using?

John and Ben work hard until the wagon is full. Then they get into the wagon and John drives close to the silo.

Ben brings a machine near the silo to cut up the corn. The machine cuts the corn, both stalk and ear, into little pieces. Then the machine blows the pieces through a pipe into the top of the silo.

Sometimes the men put clover and other green

plants into the silo. As you know, the feed in the silo is called silage. When will the farmer feed the silage to his farm animals?

Cows and sheep like silage. The green feed is kept in the silo for the animals to eat when there is no other green food for them. When the farmer takes the silage out, it smells much like pickles.

Do you see the tall windmill in the picture? When the wind blows, it turns the wheel round and round. There is a deep hole in the ground under the windmill. It is called a well. Water comes up in this hole. As the wheel turns, it works a machine which lifts water up from the well into the high water tank. The farmer needs plenty of water for his farm animals.

As the warm days go by, the corn grows fast. See the corn in this picture. How many ears can you see? See the tassels at the top of the cornstalks. The grains of corn are growing inside the green covering on the ear.

When fall comes, the cornstalks turn yellow. One day Mr. Reed tells John that they must gather the corn. The cornstalks and the ears are dry. The farmer drives his wagon into the cornfield.

His two horses walk along between the rows of corn. They pull the wagon slowly down the rows. John walks on one side of the wagon, and his father walks on the other. They turn back the husks and snap off the dry ears of corn. Quickly they toss the ears into the wagon. Then they reach for some more ears.

Up and down the field the farmer goes with the wagon. Soon the wagon is full of corn. Then John and his father climb into the wagon, and John drives to a small building near the barn.

There is an opening in the side of the building.

Mr. Reed shovels the ears of corn in through this opening. Soon there is a big pile of ears. Then John gets inside and shovels the corn away from the opening. The building has wide cracks between the boards in its sides so that the air can get in. It is called a corncrib.

When nearly all the corn is gathered, John and his father plan for some fun. They bring a few wagonloads of corn to an empty room in the barn. This corn has been snapped off the stalks, and the ears still have their husks on.

The next day Mr. Reed invites the neighbors to come for an afternoon and evening of fun. In the afternoon the young men who live on the farms near by bring their wagons and come to a corn-picking race. Jack, who lives on the next farm, won the race the year before and wants to win again. Many neighbors come to watch the corn-picking race.

The men in the race drive their empty wagons to the edge of the cornfield. They start their wagons down the rows at the same time. These rows have not been picked. Soon Jack gets ahead of all the others. He picks so fast that soon he calls to his horses to make them walk faster. Some of the neighbors follow and cheer for him. The other pickers try to catch up, but they leave some ears.

Neighbors call to them to go back and pick their rows clean. Jack wins the race, and they all go back to the house to eat the big supper which Mrs. Reed has cooked.

After supper they go to the barn for some more fun. John lights several lanterns and hangs them up on nails in the walls. He leads the way to a big room in the barn where he and his father had brought the wagonloads of ears with the husks on. Mr. Reed gives the men very large baskets and tells them to fill the baskets with ears of corn. They sit down on the floor beside their baskets and wait till he calls out "Go." The race begins.

The men grab at the ears, pull the husks back, and snap the ear off. They toss the ears into a big pile, but each man keeps the husks in a little pile beside him. When the race is over, the husks in each pile are counted. The man with the greatest number wins.

Sometimes when an ear is husked, it shows blue or red grains among the yellow. Now and then a whole ear of colored corn is found. When a man finds such an ear, everybody claps, and he gets a special prize.

WORKING ON A CORN FARM

Mr. Reed has a younger son named Ted, who likes to help his father work with their cattle. The animals which you see in the picture are cattle. Mr. Reed raises most of them to sell for meat. The meat which we get from cattle is beef. Much of the meat which we eat is beef. The cows which you have read about in another story are cattle too. For what are they raised?

After the corn has been picked in the fall, Ted lets the cattle go into the field to graze. He drives them slowly through the gate into the field. He closes the gate and goes back to the barn.

The cattle walk slowly along, taking a bite or two off one stalk and moving on to another. Sometimes they find a small ear of corn left on a stalk. They like the dry leaves and the husks too. The cattle wander about, leaving plenty of food behind them.

In the evening Ted drives the cattle back to

the yard where they are kept. He feeds more grain to them.

Mr. Reed feeds his cattle well. He wants to make them fat for the market. See the cattle eating here. Ted has put their feed into a big trough. The feed is a kind of meal which is made from corn and other grains.

The farmer bought his cattle from a big cattle ranch. They had been living in the pasture on the ranch and were not fat. All winter Mr. Reed will feed his cattle grain and silage. In the spring he will sell them for meat.

Cattle eat straw too. Did you see the big pile of straw in the last picture? It is called a strawstack. Cattle like to eat at the sides of the stack as far up as they can reach. Sometimes they eat into the stack so far that the loose, light straw falls down on them.

The farmer has one field in which he raises a grain called wheat. The straw in the big rounded stack is wheat straw. What color is the straw? Have you ever played on a strawstack?

Some farmers cut the cornstalks after the ears have been picked. They use a machine that goes

along the rows and cuts the stalks close to the ground. They pick up a few armfuls of stalks and set them on the ground with the tops up. Then they go on down the field and pile up other stacks of the corn. See what the field looks like in this picture. The stack of cornstalks is called a shock. How many shocks do you see in the picture?

Look at the picture of the cow grazing in the pasture. Mr. Reed keeps a few cows which give milk for the family to use. What else do you see besides the cow?

A cow's baby is called a calf. John has taken

care of this white-faced calf ever since it was born. At first it lived on its mother's milk. Then John took the calf away from its mother. He taught it to drink milk out of a bucket. He put his hand down into the milk and let the calf suck one of his fingers. He thought it was great fun to teach his calf to drink. John had to hold the bucket tight to keep the calf from knocking it over and spilling the milk. Before long it learned how to drink, and later it ate grass and meal feed. When it grows larger, it will eat silage.

John has taken such good care of this calf that it is a pet. When John goes into the pasture, where the calf is kept, it follows him around and likes to be petted.

Mr. Reed and his sons like to take care of the farm animals. Every day they must feed the pigs, the cattle, and the horses. They must grow plenty of feed on the farm, for they have many horses, cattle, hogs, and chickens to provide for.

The farmer grows some alfalfa for his cattle too. Alfalfa is a plant which is dried for hay. Hay is grass cut while green and then dried. Alfalfa looks much like clover. It has little round leaves and a tiny purple flower. It smells good when it is growing and blooming. When the farmer sees the blooms, he knows that the alfalfa is ready to be cut. Then he cuts the alfalfa and lets it dry. It still smells very sweet.

In the spring Mr. Reed plants vegetables for his family. He hitches a horse to a small plow and plows the garden. Then he harrows the ground and plants seeds. When weeds begin to grow in the garden, John cuts them down with a tool called a hoe. He also uses the hoe to loosen the soil around the growing vegetables.

John must also keep chickens and farm animals out of the garden. He goes over the garden often to see that bugs and worms are not eating the vegetables. All summer long the farmer's family has green vegetables from the garden. Mrs. Reed also cans some of the vegetables for winter use.

Even in winter the farmer has work to do. He puts up new fences. He looks over the barns and sheds to see what needs to be done. He sees that the farm machines are protected from the rain and snow. Every day the farm animals have to be fed and watered.

This picture shows how Mr. Reed's farm looks from the air. Find the sheds. The farmer keeps his wagons, his plows, and his other machines in the sheds.

Mr. Reed has two fields where he has planted alfalfa. Do you see these fields? Do you remember reading about the pigs? Where do they live? Why are the pigpens placed far away from the house? Find the silo, the windmill, the vegetable garden, and the fields planted in corn. Find the wheat field.

The farmer and his family live in a big white farmhouse with wide porches. Many trees grow on one side of the house. They keep high winds from blowing too hard against the house. Find the house and the trees. The farmer cuts down a few trees now and then when he needs fence posts or wood to burn, but he plants other trees to take their place. Mr. Reed has some trees from which he gets fruit. Where are these trees?

Find the road which runs past the farm. When do you think Mr. Reed and his family use this road? Would you like to live on a farm like this? Why?

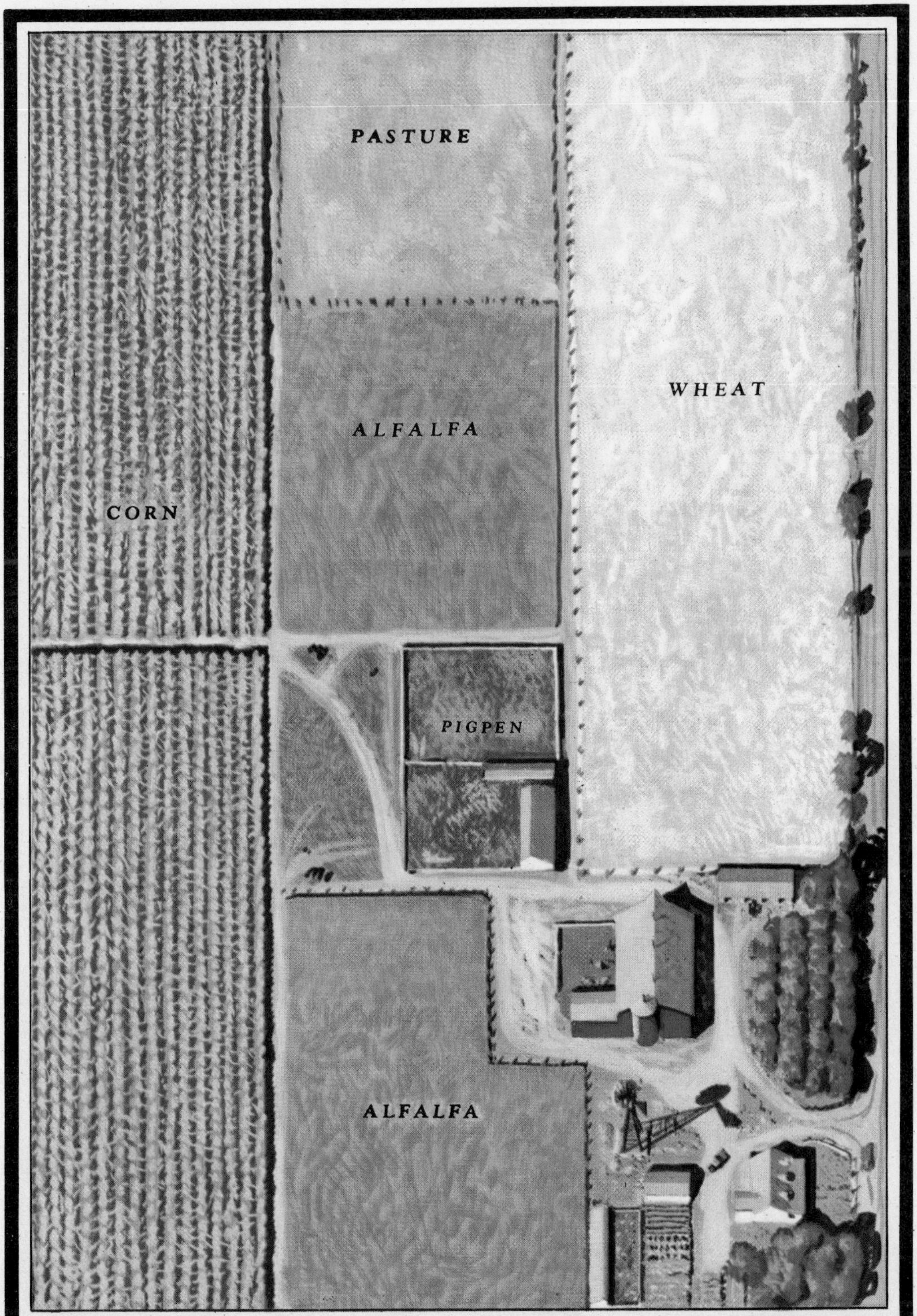

PASTURE

WHEAT

ALFALFA

CORN

PIGPEN

ALFALFA

WHAT JOHN AND MARY SAW ON THE DESERT

John and Mary Baker go with their father to visit at their grandfather's house. One day Mr. Baker takes them in his car out into the desert. John and Mary have never seen a desert and wonder what it is like.

After they have left town, the children watch to see whether they can tell when they come to the desert. When their father tells them that the desert is just ahead, they see bare, dry land. It is level land and stretches far away to the mountains. There are no houses. There are no people. It is quiet, and the sun is very bright.

Then Mr. Baker stops the car. When the children get out, it is so warm that they take off their sweaters. John asks why this land is called a desert. His father tells him that it is a dry place where few plants can grow.

The children see only bushes and a few small trees. Almost all of the bushes grow far apart. There is bare ground around most of the bushes and trees.

Mr. Baker tells the children that plants in such a dry land need much space to send out their roots. Each root will find only a little water, or moisture, in the soil. The plants also have long roots that go deep down in the ground for water. Unless the roots bring enough water to the plant, it will die.

John and Mary are surprised to find any plants growing in the desert. The land looks so dry that

the children do not see how a plant can find enough moisture to live.

See the trees which grow on the desert. Mr. Baker tells the children that they are Joshua trees. The branches look like short arms reaching out at you. After the spring rains on the desert, big white blossoms come out on the Joshua tree.

Mr. Baker drives a long way to another part of the desert. He wants to show the children a different kind of desert land where it is much warmer. He leaves the paved road and drives over dirt roads. It is very dusty, and the car is soon covered with dust.

This spring there have been many rains. The rains have poured down just a short time ago. The spring flowers have come up very quickly after the rain.

Mary and John are glad that they can see some of the desert flowers. These flowers are very bright in color, red and blue and yellow. Most of them grow in little bunches close to the ground.

What color are the flowers which you see in this picture? What do we call these desert trees?

After the rains the flowers bloom only a short

time. Soon they go to seed and dry up. People who want to see the desert in bloom have to go there at the right time. If they are a little too late, they will not see the flowers. After the flowers have withered away, the desert is dry and bare again. You would not guess that flowers had ever grown there.

John and Mary have seen movies of a desert, but they do not know where that desert is. They have seen camels and Arabs traveling over sandy places. But they look all around on this desert and can see no camels or Arabs. Their father says that camels and Arabs do not live in our

country. The deserts where Arabs live are in another country far away from ours. Those deserts look different from this one, for, you see, not all deserts are alike.

Soon John sees a place in the desert where hardly any plants are growing. There are no trees to be seen. The ground is very dry. See this bare place in the picture.

John asks his father why nothing grows there. Mr. Baker says that once salt water had covered this place. When the water dried up, salt was left behind in the soil. Such a place is called a dry lake.

Plants will not grow there because of the salt in the soil.

The children are glad to know about dry lakes. John plans to play a joke on his chum at school. He will ask what a lake is. When the chum says that it is a body of water, John will say that sometimes it is nothing but dry land.

Then Mary sees some bushes which are almost as tall as a man. They are very dark green and have many branches coming up from the same spot on the ground. These bushes grow far apart like most of the desert plants. They cannot get enough moisture from the soil if they grow close together.

By this time Mary asks if all of the desert land is dry. Her father says that it is too dry in most places for men to raise vegetables, grains, or other plants for food. It is too dry to raise sheep. The sheep could not find enough to eat.

Then Mr. Baker drives on to a place in the desert where many plants are growing. See the stream of water in the picture. See the green plants. People live here and have water for their fields. It is a green spot in the middle of the desert.

The stream starts up in the mountains. As it

comes down to the level land, it soaks into the dry ground. It gets smaller and smaller. Then it dries up.

Green plants grow near the stream. But just a little way from the stream the land is dry. You can tell just where the water is by the green plants. There are only a few places on the desert where there is water. People must have water to drink. They cannot live in a desert or anywhere else unless they can get enough water.

Sometimes people dig a deep hole in the ground to get water. When they find water coming into the hole, they stop digging. What is such a hole called? If the water is very far down in the ground, people must use a machine called a drill to make the hole.

Sometimes people find places in the desert where water comes out from the side of a hill or bubbles up on top of the ground. Do you know what such a place is called?

If enough water can be carried to the desert land, people can make farms there. They can raise cattle, and many people can make their homes there.

ANIMALS THAT LIVE ON THE DESERT

As Mr. Baker drives along the desert road, John asks why he has not seen any animals. Is it too dry for animals to live in the desert?

Mr. Baker stops the car at the side of the road and tells the children to watch. If they look carefully, they may be able to see animals hiding in the bushes.

Just then the children see a jack rabbit with long ears leaping across the level land. He jumps right over the low bushes. Then he sits up on his hind legs and looks off across the desert. He holds his long ears up straight, as if he were listening.

While the children watch, the rabbit begins to eat the thorny bush which is beside him. It is called a cactus. If you touch the cactus, sharp thorns will hurt your hands. But the rabbit knows how to get his food from the cactus plant. Mr. Baker says that the jack rabbit likes the juice which is inside. The outside of the cactus is dry and hard. But the inside is juicy like a fruit. It is both food and drink for the rabbit.

The children keep very still. The rabbit has not seen them yet, and they do not want to scare him away.

If a jack rabbit lives near a green place on the desert where people raise a garden, he is almost sure to get into trouble. He will know where the plants are growing. He will nibble the green leaves and hurt the plants and fruit trees. He may get caught.

There are other desert animals which would like to eat the jack rabbit. The wild dog, or coyote, is one of the rabbit's enemies. The coyote can run fast and chase the rabbits. When a rabbit is in danger, he lays his ears back and runs. He does not need to hear then.

The coyote also likes to catch the desert squirrels and mice. But the smaller animals do not go far away from their holes. When they see a coyote, they run for a hole and dive in.

Coyotes do not like to come near people. But people who camp on the desert at night often hear the cry of the coyote. It makes a strange sound that is very much like a dog's howling or a baby's crying.

Mary is the first to see a horned toad. It runs near a low bush and looks so much like the ground that John says he does not see the toad. Can you see it in the picture? Its back is spotted to make it look like the ground.

Mary wants to catch the little toad. But it runs away very fast. It does not want to be caught. After it stops running, it stays very still. If it had moved, John might have seen it.

The children see many little holes in the ground where desert squirrels and mice live. When a larger animal is chasing them, they run very fast and hide in their holes. They store food in the ground and usually stay there during the hottest part of the day.

See the lizard which lives in the desert. Mr. Baker caught it after it ran across the road and went up on a flat rock. It has four short legs and can run so fast that you can hardly see it. It hides among the rocks or under bushes. See its long tail. What color is the lizard?

When a lizard scampers across the road in front of your automobile, you expect it to be killed. But it runs so fast that it gets away.

The children ask how the animals can live in the desert where it is so hot and dry in the summer. Mr. Baker says that the animals come out of their holes and hiding places at night when it is cooler. He tells the children that there would be more animals if there were plenty of water.

Many different kinds of birds live on the desert. They eat insects and the seeds of the desert plants. Often they build their nests in a big cactus. The thorny sides of the cactus keep other animals away from the birds' nests. How do you think the birds get a drink of water? They peck into the cactus for water.

The children wear thin clothes while they are watching for animals. The day is warm. The wind is blowing hard, and it is dusty too.

Soon after sunset it gets chilly. The children have to put on their warm sweaters. They are glad to get into the car out of the wind. Mr. Baker turns the car around and drives back to grandfather's house and a good supper.

WHAT IS A PLAIN?

Most people live on level land. Such land is called a plain. The land is not as smooth or as flat as the top of a table, but it does not have high hills. It does not have mountains. Because the land is level, it is easy to drive over.

On most of the level land in our country there is enough rain to make plants grow. Where the soil is good, the farmers can raise fruits and vegetables easily. Many streams flow through these level lands. At times there is so much water in the streams that the water runs out over the land.

The level land in other parts of our country has forests growing on it. Other level land has green grass on which animals graze.

Some of the level land is cold in winter. Winds blow, and deep snow falls. Often wind and snow come at the same time. Sometimes such strong winds come that houses are blown down.

Fun on the Lake

PLAYING AT THE LAKE

One morning William puts on his cap and goes to see his friend Tom. The boys are spending their vacation at a lake. They walk along the lake, stopping now and then to throw stones into the water. They see the ripples spread away from the spot when the stone hits the water.

Tom has just thrown a stone. It flew through the air. Can you see where the stone fell? The boys heard it when it hit the water. It said "klump." There was a big splash which sent ripples out on the water. The ripples became smaller as they spread.

After a while the boys become tired of throwing stones. Then they take a walk through the shady forest beside the lake. There are many pine trees in the forest. The ground is covered with pine needles which have fallen from the trees. The boys run and slide on the pine needles. They like the piny smell of the trees.

Soon the boys come to another lake where some of their friends are swimming. A little boy is diving off a board into the water. How does he hold his arms when he dives?

Near the edge, or shore, of the lake the water is not deep. How high does it come up on the little girl with light hair? See the girl lying on the red rubber float. She kicks her feet and moves through the water. The rubber float holds the girl up.

Tom and William want to go into the water too. There is a little bathhouse where they change clothes and put on their swimming suits. The man at the bathhouse shows them where the deep water begins.

The boys go running down to the shore and into the water. Tom starts swimming out into the lake. But William stays near the shore because he cannot swim.

Tom lies still in the water with only his face showing and looks up at the blue sky. He moves along slowly. You see, Tom knows how to float. After a while he wishes that William were out in the middle of the lake with him.

Tom swims back to the place where William is wading. He takes William out where the water is deeper but not over their heads. Then Tom begins to teach William how to float on his back. William wants to learn how to swim, but Tom tells him to learn to float first. Tom puts one hand under William's head and the other under his back. Soon William learns to lie still and let the water hold him up. Then Tom tells him to kick with his feet, and William finds he can move slowly along. He likes to float. He will soon learn to swim.

GOING BOATING

Today some of the children go out on the water in Tom's red canoe. Tom's sister Dorothy sits at the front with a paddle in her hand. Tom at the other end also has a paddle. Two of their friends sit on the other seats of the canoe.

Dorothy and Tom make the canoe move slowly through the water. They dip the paddles in the water and push back. Then they lift the paddles out and dip them in again. The children like to paddle along the shore and around to the other side of the lake.

A canoe will upset easily. But all the children in this canoe can swim. What kind of clothes are they wearing? Why are they dressed in this way?

The children who cannot swim do not go out in a canoe. Their fathers take them out on the lake in other kinds of boats. After they learn to swim, they can ride in canoes too.

As Tom paddles along, he sees his father out on the lake in a boat. Tom's father makes this boat go not with paddles but with oars. One oar is fastened on each side of the boat. It is called a rowboat. Another man is in the boat with Tom's father.

Tom knows that the men are fishing. They throw a line into the water. Soon they feel a fish pulling at the end of the line. Since it is a small fish, the men easily pull it into the boat. Next they catch a large fish. They work for a long time to pull it in. Tom hopes his father will catch many fish. Then he can give his friends some fish for their suppers.

From the canoe the children see the sailboat which is in this picture. How many people are in this sailboat? What color are the sails? The wind blows against the sails. Then the boat moves in the water. The people in the boat know how to turn the sails in different ways. Then they can make the boat go the way they want it to go.

Tom and Dorothy call to their friends on the sailboat. Their friends answer and wave to the children.

Toward evening the children paddle back to shore. They get out of the canoe and draw it up on the shore. Then they run home to tell about the good time they had out on the water. They wonder when supper will be ready.

Dorothy and Tom reach the house in the woods where they live. It is made of logs and is called a cabin. They get washed and dressed for supper.

Dorothy is ready before Tom is. She comes out to the campfire where the rest of the family are. See Dorothy's mother and father in the picture. Her big sister is wearing a red waist. There is a

cool breeze this evening and Dorothy comes close to the fire to warm her hands.

For a little while Dorothy stands with the others waiting while the wood in the fire burns away and becomes glowing coals.

The children's father has cleaned the fish and brought them to the cabin. Their mother rolls them in meal, salts them, and puts them into the frying pan. They sizzle in the hot grease and are soon browned. Then the father jerks the frying pan so that the fish are turned over. Now they cook on the other side.

Soon Tom comes and helps too. He watches the coffeepot to keep it from boiling over. It sits at the edge of the fire. When the food is ready, Tom brings wood and builds up the fire until it is blazing again.

Then all the family sit around the fire and eat their supper. The fire gives them light and warms them as they eat. They toss the fishbones into the flames.

Soon after supper the girls wash the dishes. Tom helps put away the food. Tom is yawning. Mother says it is time for the children to go to bed.

WALKING AROUND THE LAKES

One morning May and Jim start on a long walk. They have heard the older boys and girls talk about walking around the lakes. May and Jim decide that they will walk around the lakes too. They are wearing their swimming suits.

First the children go around a big lake. It takes them nearly all morning to come back to the place where they started.

Then they come to the biggest lake, but they know that they cannot walk around it. When May and Jim look across it, they can barely see the other side.

As the children hike, they see some small ponds. They walk all around a small lake in a few minutes. Then they run a race along the shore of the lake. May gets off the path and hits her toe on the root of a tree. Jim tells her to put her foot in the cool water. The two children sit down at the edge of

the little lake with their feet hanging over and splashing back and forth in the water. Then the children start off again. They have taken long walks every day during vacation and do not get tired.

Jim sees some land out in one of the lakes. Water is all around this bit of land. It is called an island. May says that she is going to ask her mother to let the children have a picnic on the island. Jim says that his big brother will take the children out to the island in his boat. May and Jim think they would like to go to the island the next day. They hurry home to ask whether they may have a picnic on the island.

This drawing shows the path May and Jim took when they walked around the lakes. The drawing shows how the land would look from up in the air above the lakes. The lakes are blue. How many lakes do you see?

Find the place where the children started. Where is the little lake the children walked around in only a few minutes? Find the island where the children wanted to have a picnic. How do you know that this land is an island?

BIG LAKE

BIGGEST LAKE

WINTER AT THE LAKE

Elizabeth and her little brother Sam have come to the lake for a winter holiday. It is a bright, cold day. The pine trees around the lake are green, but they are covered with snow. The snow on the branches is so heavy that it bends the trees down. Snow covers the ground too.

See the children on their sled sliding down a hill to the lake. They are warm, for they have on their snow suits. What color is Sam's suit? It has a warm hood on it and covers him from head to foot. Elizabeth does not wear a cap, but she has ear muffs on.

The sled goes whizzing down the hill. The hill is slippery, and the boys and girls like to have the sled go fast. The children hold fast to the sled so that they will not fall off. When it reaches the lake, they shout. Now it runs smoothly over the ice

far out to the middle of the lake. When it stops, the children get off, laughing and shouting.

They start back toward the hill with the sled. But the ice is slippery. Sam tries to run and slide, and then he takes a tumble. He tries to get up, but his feet go out from under him, and he falls down again. Elizabeth holds on to the sled and reaches out to help him up. His coat is covered with snow and bits of ice when he gets up. Elizabeth helps him brush it off. The children walk carefully on the ice.

At last they reach the hill again. But they do

not pull their sled up the steep slope. Elizabeth leads the way up a gentle slope through soft snow. It is easier to go up that way. Then Elizabeth and Sam get on the sled and go whizzing down again.

After a while Sam wants to skate. The children take the sled back to the house. Then they put on their skating shoes which they had left under a tree. They stand up on their skates and walk slowly out on the ice. Off they go on their skates. Other boys and girls are skating too. Maybe you can find Elizabeth and Sam among the skaters. How will you know them?

Sam and Elizabeth have to be good skaters to skate on this lake. The ice is like glass today. The children dart around the lake. Some skate alone, and others skate together.

In one part of the lake there is a sign which says "Keep off." The ice is not thick there. The children know that it is not safe to skate on thin ice. One boy is skating too fast to turn away when he comes to the thin ice. He hears a cracking sound under him and dashes away as fast as he can go.

One of the older boys has an iceboat. It moves

by catching wind in the sails. You can see that it is on runners. The boy and his friends lie flat on the boat and move the sails to catch the wind. In the iceboat they slide swiftly over the ice. Have you ever seen an iceboat like this one?

After a while some of the children stop skating. They gather branches which have fallen from the trees. The boys shake the snow off this firewood and build a fire on the shore. It blazes up, and the children crowd around it to warm their hands and feet. Sam goes as close to the fire as he can. Do you see him? The children are laughing and

talking about the skating games they will play on the ice.

By this time the cold air has made the children hungry. Some of the older boys and girls begin to cook food over the fire. One girl makes hot chocolate. Another puts sausages in a big skillet. Someone brings out a package of bread, already cut and buttered. Each child takes a piece and holds it out for the cook to put a steaming sausage on it. The hot chocolate is poured. How good all the food tastes!

The boys and girls stand around the fire eating.

More firewood is brought, for the children are getting cold. They are not moving about now as they were when they were skating and sliding.

Soon it is time to start for home. One of the bigger boys sees that the children do not forget their skates or sweaters or scarfs. They have had a good time playing in the snow and on the ice. But now they want to go home.

Do you think that you would like to go to the lake in winter? Or would you have more fun there in the summer? Why? What would you do at the lake in winter?

WHAT IS A LAKE?

Sometimes water gathers in a hollow in the land. If the hollow is small, we call the water a pond. But if water gathers in a big hollow, we call the place a lake.

In the hills water may come out from the ground. Often this water runs down into a hollow and makes a lake.

People like to go to lakes for the summer because it is often cool near the shore. They may visit small lakes or lakes so large you cannot see across them. How do people enjoy themselves at the lake? Have you ever seen a lake?

Often the water from a lake flows into a stream. Sometimes that stream is wide, and sometimes it is narrow. If a big lake flows into a stream, the stream is usually a river.

Sometimes a lake is made by men. How can they do it? A wall called a dam is built across the stream. The wall comes to an end where the land is high enough to keep the water back. The water cannot get past the wall. If the dam were not there, most of the water would flow away.

In a lake there may be a piece of land with water all around it. It may be a big piece of land or a very small piece.

Some islands in lakes are so large that people build their homes on them. Others are too bare and rocky for people to live on. Men cannot have farms on such lands. Are there any islands near the place where you live?

River Stories

CUTTING TREES INTO LOGS

One morning just after breakfast Mrs. Smith asks her husband what he is going to do today. It is a bright, sunny day, and she hopes that he will work outdoors. Ben Smith tells her that he must pick out the trees in his forest which his helpers are to cut down. He takes a hatchet and goes to the forest. Since the day is warm, he does not wear a coat over his blue shirt.

See Ben marking a tree with his hatchet. He makes a little cut in the side of the tree. Then the men will know that he wants this tree cut down. It is a big tree. When it is gone, the small trees around it will have more space to grow.

Mr. Smith grows trees so that he can sell the logs. He sells them to a man who runs a mill. At this mill some of the wood is made into lumber. Other wood is ground up to make paper. The bark is taken off. Then the inside of the log is ground into little bits. Soon you will see how Ben gets the logs down to the mill. You will see how the inside wood of the logs is used.

After Ben has marked a tree, two men come to cut it down. One of them takes his ax and chops into the side of the tree to mark the way they want it to fall. They will make the tree fall where there is space for it. If the tree fell the wrong way, it might break the young trees near by.

Then the men begin sawing from the other side of the tree. How many men hold the saw? Where do they begin to saw on the tree? Why do they cut Ben's tree so close to the ground?

When the men have sawed part way through the tree, they know it is nearly ready to fall. They hear it begin to break away, and they call "Timber!" Their call tells the other men that a tree is about to fall.

Several men are busy cutting down trees in Ben's forest. The forest is large, and two men could not do all the work.

Ben hears the men call "Timber!" and stops his work to look at the tree on the ground. He measures it with a stick. He talks with the men about cutting

the tree into logs. See them sawing the tree trunk into logs.

How long is the saw which the men use? Do you think it will take a long time for them to saw through the trunk?

There is a stream of water, or river, near Ben's forest. The men will take the logs to the river. The men use horses to drag the logs toward the river. Ben works hard helping the men. These men have worked for him for many years. Every year they go into the forest to cut down some of the larger trees.

Look at this picture. Do you see how the men get the logs to the river? The horses are strong and can pull heavy logs. But most of the logs are not big.

When the men come near the river, they pile up the logs on the bank. All day long Ben and his men work sawing tree trunks and bringing logs to the river. They are careful not to hurt any of the young trees in the forest. When these trees have more space, they will grow big too.

When the men have cut down enough trees, they will send the logs down to the mill.

FLOATING THE LOGS DOWN THE RIVER

One morning Mr. Smith gets up early and eats a big breakfast. His wife puts up a good lunch for him. What work do you think he is going to do?

Ben calls two men to help him. They go toward the river. It is a bright, sunny day and Ben knows that he will enjoy his work.

When they reach the river, the men go to the place where a long, narrow boat is tied to a tree. It is a wooden boat somewhat like the canoes which you have read about. Mr. Smith and the men will need the boat while they are taking the logs to the mill.

In the boat are some long poles, each with a hook at one end. Ben gives each man a pole. Soon you will see how the men use these poles.

Now Ben goes to a pile of logs and pushes a log toward the river. The log rolls down the bank. See it go splashing into the stream! What happens

when the log touches the water? One log after another goes down into the river. Water splashes up on the banks and makes the place muddy. But the men keep working with their poles, trying to make the logs turn the right way.

Soon all the logs are in the river. The men take their long poles and step out on the logs. They know how to stand on a floating log without falling off. They keep their feet moving all the time they are on the log. You see they have learned how to stand up on a log and help keep all the logs moving.

The men begin to guide the logs down the river. They reach out with their poles to make the logs go the right way.

As the men turn the logs, some of the bark is torn away. When the logs reach the mill, the rest of the bark will be taken off.

After all the logs have started down the river, the men get into their boat. Ben says that they must go with the logs to keep them moving toward the mill.

Can you see how the men move the boat? See the big rock in the river. What has happened to the logs near the rock? Ben pushes them downstream with his pole. The other men help him. The river flows fast. It carries the logs along with it.

As the men guide the boat downstream, they see that logs have piled up against a big rock near the shore. More logs float against the pile and get

caught. The three men step out on to the logs and move about the pile. They want to see which logs keep the others from moving.

Ben sees where the logs are caught on the rock. When he pulls them away, the other logs which are caught there float on down the river.

It is evening by the time the men reach the mill with the logs. They leave the logs in a quiet pond near the mill. They have worked too fast to get cold, but now they are wet and hungry. They will be glad to get home and put on dry clothes. Then they will eat a good dinner.

AT THE MILL

The mill to which Mr. Smith brought his logs is owned by Will Blake. There is a pond near the mill where Will keeps the logs until he is ready to use them.

The mill stands at the edge of the river. The moving water turns the big mill wheel. When this wheel runs it makes a big saw cut the logs up. Mr. Blake built his mill beside the river so that the moving water could help him in this way. He also uses a great deal of water in getting the wood ready to make paper.

Will looks over the logs in his pond. A few of them are big. He tells his men to cut these big logs into boards. But most of the logs are too small to make boards. Mr. Blake will grind up these small logs.

The fine bits of wood are soaked in water. They get soft and make a thick soup called wood pulp.

It is used to make paper. Perhaps the paper on which you write is made of wood pulp.

Here is one of Mr. Blake's men at work. Do you see the big log? It still has the bark on. What is being done to this log? Where is the saw which is cutting the log up? What makes the saw move?

The men in the mill are busy. What else will they need to do when the log is cut into boards?

If Ben's forest were not up the river, he could not float his logs down to Mr. Blake's mill. He would have to send the logs by trucks or by flatcars on a railroad train. Have you ever seen a flatcar? It

would cost Ben much more to send his logs to the mill by truck or train. Then he would not make so much money from his trees.

In the winter Ben cannot float his logs down to the mill. The river is frozen over during part of the winter. Sometimes Ben cuts down the trees in winter and piles the logs up until spring comes. When the ice has melted, he and his men push the logs into the river. Then the logs float down to the mill.

Many of the forests in our country are far away from a river. Their owners cannot send logs to a mill by floating. How will they get their logs there?

Here is a picture which shows what the land looks like from the air. It shows Mr. Blake's mill and the forest and the river. Where is Ben's forest? Where is the mill? Can you tell which way this river flows? How do you know? Find a little stream which runs into the river. Where did the logs pile up in the river? Such a pile of logs is called a log jam. Why did the logs stop there? What did the men do to help move the logs?

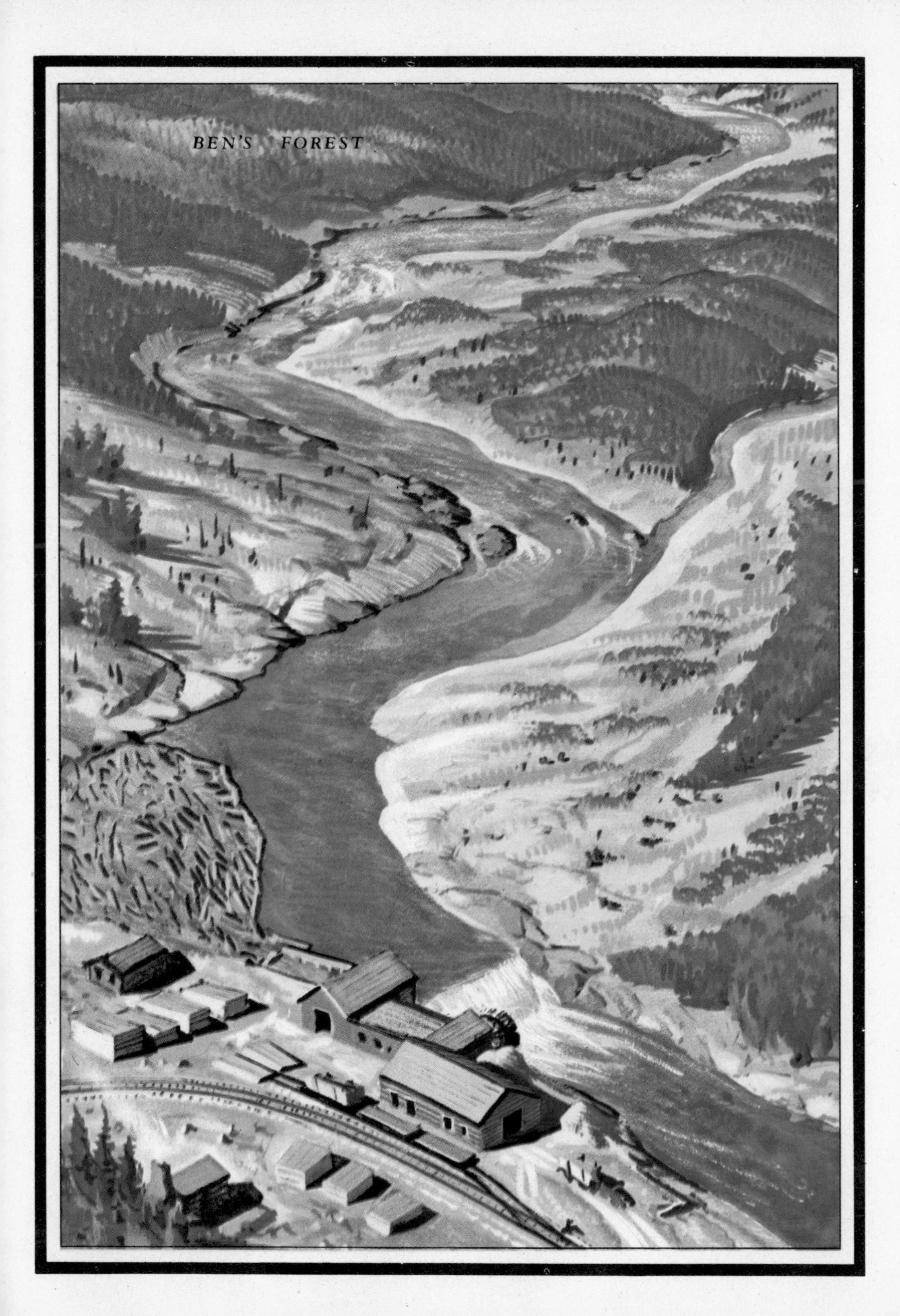
BEN'S FOREST

WHAT IS A RIVER?

The river about which you have been reading starts up on high land. At first it is a little stream. Since the land is hilly, the stream runs down the hill. Other little streams flow into it. It gets larger and larger.

Rivers always flow downhill. Water cannot flow up. If you will put some water on the side of a slope, you will see that it will flow down. Every river in the world flows down.

Sometimes a river winds around and flows into another river. Many rivers run to a big body of water called the sea.

Some rivers move slowly, and others flow fast. A river may flow so fast that it will cut away the land. Some rivers have clear water, and others are so muddy that the water looks brown. Some rivers are long, and others are short. Some are wide, and others are narrow.

Sea Stories

AT THE BEACH

Nancy is spending her vacation at the seashore. She is a little girl with straight yellow hair. Nancy and her two little brothers have come with their mother to the beach because it is cool there in the summer.

The children go down to the shore to play. The water which you see is the sea, or ocean. Nancy looks out over the ocean. It is so large that she cannot see where the water ends. The waves from the ocean wash up on the shore. The sandy part of the shore which is washed by the waves is called a beach. Cool breezes nearly always blow in from the ocean.

The sand near the edge of the water is wet and hard. But when Nancy walks on the dry beach away from the water, her feet slip down into the deep sand. Soon there is sand in her shoes and in Bob's shoes and in Tim's shoes. It is hard for the

children to walk because their feet sink down into the dry sand. The children sit down and take off their shoes. They shake out the sand, and then put on their shoes again. When they walk on the hard, wet sand, the sand does not get into their shoes.

That afternoon the children come back to play in the sand. What has Nancy brought to play with? The children feel the warm sun on their bare legs. The sand is warm. Tim picks up some sand and lets it run between his fingers.

But the children do not sit still very long. They want to run along the beach and find some of their friends. Tim walks on one side of Nancy, and Bob on the other.

The children see bright orange and green umbrellas stuck down in the sand. When the people are not in swimming, they like to lie on the sand. Some of them lie in the sun on big bath towels. A few children have bright tin pails and shovels. They dig deep holes and shovel the sand into their pails. Nancy and her brothers take off their shoes and socks and wade out a little way into the water.

Then Nancy stands on the beach and looks out at

the ocean. The water is moving all the time. As it goes up and down, it makes waves. Most of the waves are not very big until they get close to the shore. Then they get higher and higher, and finally the top of the wave rolls over and breaks. Nancy watches the waves break. The water gets foamy and white as it falls. We call a breaking wave a breaker. Some of the waves break right at the shore.

Some big boys and girls are wading out to meet a big wave. They jump up as the wave reaches them. It carries them a little way and goes on to break on the shore.

Small children can easily be knocked down by a breaker. Strong grown-up swimmers go out beyond the breakers because the water is more quiet.

Nancy and her brothers find some friends. The boys begin building a sand tower. Then Nancy slips away to a little house up on the beach. It is just a tiny room with a bench along one wall. Nancy's swimming suit is hanging in this bathhouse. Nancy puts on the suit and fastens a white rubber cap over her hair to keep it dry.

See Nancy as she steps into the water. The water seems cold when she first walks into it. She

shivers a little at first, for the water is cooler than the air. Then she wades out beyond the breakers and begins to swim. After she has been swimming a little while, the water does not seem cold.

In the place where Nancy swims, the breakers are not big. When a big breaker comes in, she gets a mouthful of water. The water is salty, and Nancy does not like the taste.

After a while she comes to shore and runs along the beach to the place where Bob and Tim are playing. She lies in the sand. Bob digs his hands down into the sand and piles the sand up all around her. Soon only her head is showing. Bob heaps the sand up and pats it down until she looks like a little hill of sand. But Nancy does not like this. She sits up and looks off at the water.

Nancy sees that the waves are washing far up on the beach. Each time the water comes in, it seems to wash up a little higher. The boys and girls who are sitting in the sand close to the water move higher up on the beach. The dry sand is getting wet now. The children do not have so much space to play in. Nancy tells Bob and Tim that the tide is coming in. She says it is high tide.

Nancy likes to swim when the tide is high. Then when she runs out into the ocean, there is smooth sand under her feet. Sometimes the water is high up on the beach in the morning, and sometimes it is high up in the afternoon.

Nancy and the boys decide to go home. The waves have washed away the tower which the boys built. The sandy beach is nearly covered with water now. Two other girls who are waiting for their mothers stay and watch the breakers rolling toward the shore. But they will soon go away too.

AT LOW TIDE

Sometimes Nancy and her brothers go down to the ocean when the sand is nearly all wet. The waves are not coming high up on the beach. People say that it is low tide. The children have to walk a long way out to reach the water.

The little boys take their dog along with them. They throw a ball for the dog to run after. The dog runs over the wet sand where the water has been. Rover likes to go into the water. He is a good swimmer. When the boys throw the ball out into the waves, he swims after it.

While the boys play with the dog, Nancy looks for shells in the sand. When the water was high, it left shells on the beach. Nancy sees a little shell shining in the sunlight. She picks it up and looks at the pretty red marks on the outside of the shell. It is half of a shell that a little sea animal used to live in.

The children see many little holes in the sand. Tiny bugs and worms have made these holes as they dug down into the sand. They come up out of the sand when the waves wash in. Bob shovels quickly hoping to see a sand worm. Surely enough he sees it, but it digs down in the sand again before he can pick it up.

Tim finds a long piece of seaweed which was washed up on the beach. He drags the seaweed after him as he runs. It is still wet and shines in the sun. Rover runs after Tim and bites at the seaweed. This brown weed grows in the ocean.

Sometimes pieces of seaweed are broken off and are washed in by the waves.

The children come to a part of the beach where there are little hills of dry sand. The wind blows it about and heaps the sand up in big piles. Rough grass grows on some of the hills. Tell how high the water will go up on this beach at the time of high tide.

Bob and Rover run on ahead of the others. Soon Bob comes to some big rocks and climbs up on them. Rover jumps up too. Up on these high rocks Bob looks far out to sea. He sees a boat far out on the water. Then he looks up and down the shore. Not far away he sees the round tower which is in this picture. There is a big light at the top of the tower. At night this light shines out to sea. It guides the sailors so that they can keep their ships off the rocks along the coast. This tower with its big light is called a lighthouse. Bob thinks that he would like to climb up in the tower to see the light. He would also like to see it moving over the sky at night.

Bob looks at the rocks and sees little pools of water left by the waves. The rocks are covered with tiny shells. In each shell lives a tiny animal.

Bob calls to Tim and Nancy to come to the place which he has found. The two children hurry to catch up with him. They climb up on the high rocks.

Then all three children begin to look at the little animals in a pool. Tim finds a little animal fastened to the rock but sees that it does not have a shell. It looks like a flower in bloom. This little animal is pale pink, but another like it is yellow. Each leaf waves in the water to catch food. Tim reaches down into the water to touch the little animal. It closes up. Then he cannot see any color, for the little animal looks like the rock which it grows on.

Nancy finds a big pool of water with many little shells in it. She sees a green crab come out of a crack in the rocks. The crab has many legs and moves fast. Nancy holds a stick close to it to see whether it will take hold of the stick. But the crab runs back into the crack in the rocks. Then Nancy cannot see it because it is hiding among the wet rocks.

Tim and Nancy look up and down the shore. They see sandy beaches and other places where

there are high rocks much like those that they are standing on.

The children are careful to leave the rocks before the tide gets high again. If the children were to stay too long, the water might fill the low places near the shore. Then they would find it hard to get back to land.

Nancy, Bob, and Tim gather up the shells which they have found. They have had a good time at the beach and are glad to be going home. Tim takes his seaweed along, and Rover races ahead of them barking.

THE SEASHORE IN WINTER

It is wintertime at the beach where Nancy and her brothers played. There are no people on the beach. The skies are gray. The water is rough because a strong wind is blowing in from the sea.

The ocean is not frozen over as a lake or river might be at this time of year. The ocean water is salty and must be much colder than fresh water to freeze. People do not go skating on the ocean.

See the beach on which the children played last summer. How does it look now? The children would not get their shoes full of sand if they walked on the beach now. How do you think it would feel to walk on this beach in winter?

Even though it is winter, the tide keeps coming in and going out. Twice every day the tide comes in and goes out. The waves still break on the beach, and the water is always moving back and forth.

It is windy and cold on the beach today. Off in the distance there are little waves of foam on the water. They are called whitecaps. The wind has made the waves break into foam.

There are no visitors at the seashore now. But the children who live near the shore all year round often walk on the beach. They run races on the hard sand. They come to the beach often to see whether the waves have washed up any shells or seaweed. In a storm they like to stand and watch the big waves sweep up and break on the beach. The noise is like thunder.

See the rocks on which Nancy played last summer. Far up from the water's edge the rocks are covered with ice and snow. Close to the water, where the waves dash over them, they are slippery. It would not be safe to walk on them.

Every wave sends fine drops of water, or spray, up on the rocks. As the waves wash in and out, they move the loose sand back and forth. But the waves cannot move the rocks that go deep down into the ground. The waves carry sand away and pile it up in other places. The beach will look very different next summer.

FISHERMEN AT SEA

Joe Carter and Fred Brown are fishermen. They live near the ocean and work for the captain of a fishing boat. This afternoon Joe and Fred are getting their fishing lines ready.

The fishing lines are long, for they must reach deep into the sea. Each line has many little lines hanging from it. At the end of each little line there is a hook. On each hook Joe and Fred will put food for the fish to bite.

They take a big fish and cut it up into little bits. Then they put a bit of the fish on each hook. The food which is put on a fishhook is called bait. The fish in the sea will try to eat the bait and will get caught on the hook. It takes Joe and Fred a long time to put bait on all the hooks. They carefully put each baited line around the inside of a tub.

That night the captain and his fishermen start

out to sea. They go in a boat that is moved by sails. See Fred and Joe getting on the boat. Fred goes first, carrying a bundle of clothes which he will need. Joe follows Fred. Joe is an old man with white hair. He has gone to sea many times. The sky is dark, and it is cold. But the men are dressed warm and do not feel the cold.

The men start out at night, for they want to reach the fishing grounds by morning. The place where they will fish is far out at sea. It will take them many hours to get there. The sails fill with air, and the boat moves fast.

After the men leave shore, there is water all around them. It is easy to get lost on the ocean. But the sailors can tell when they are going the right way. A little later in this story, you will learn how they tell which way the boat is going.

The boat has an engine, but the sailors like to sail when there is a good wind. Tonight the wind is blowing hard and tips the boat far over to one side. Water washes over the floor, or deck. Spray fills the air. It hits the men's faces and tastes salty on their lips. Their faces have already been tanned by the wind and the sun.

See Fred turning the big red wheel. He is making the fishing boat go in the right way, or steering it. The captain gave him orders about which way to go. As he steers, he looks down into a lighted box. The box has a face with the directions marked on it. This face which turns around and around always shows where each direction is. Fred looks at this compass to know which way to turn the wheel. Fred is wearing rubber boots and a short, heavy coat. It is damp and chilly at the wheel. Fred hears the sails of the boat flapping in the wind as the boat is turned.

After a while it is Fred's turn to sleep. Another

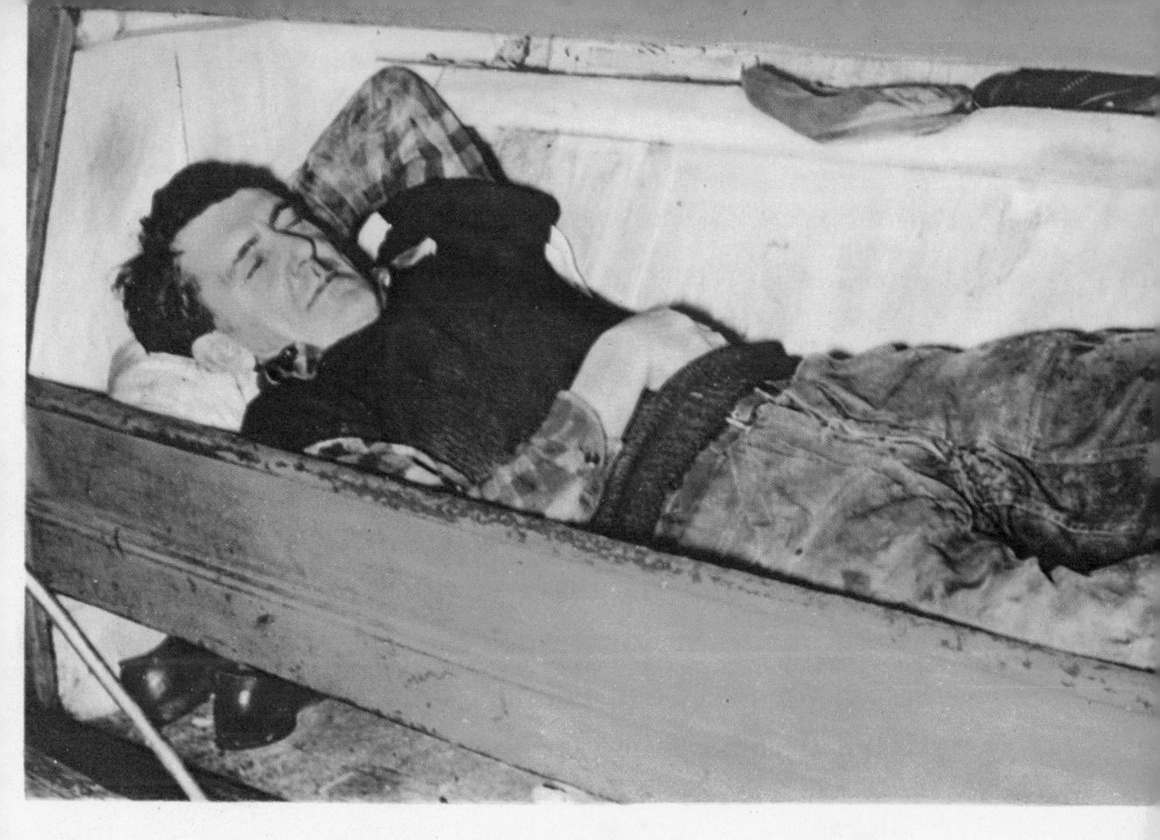

man takes his place. Fred goes down inside the boat where beds are built against the walls. There are not many beds, for only a few of the sailors sleep at a time.

Fred takes off his boots and goes to sleep in his clothes. There is a light near the bunk, but Fred can sleep with the light shining on him.

The boat rocks on the water, and the waves slap against the side of the boat. But Fred is tired and goes to sleep at once. He sleeps when he can because he must work in the morning.

Early the next morning the sun shines bright on

the ocean. The boat has reached the place where the men will fish. Now they are very busy. On the deck are rowboats, or dories, which the men will fish from. Fred gets into one of these little boats holding a small barrel which he will need. Other men lower the boat into the water. Do you see these men? How are they dressed? Why? Joe will go out in this boat with Fred. Two men fish from each little boat. How many little boats can you see? Some of the other men have already put their boats into the water. Some of them are on the way to where they will fish.

Joe and Fred row away in their dory. Which man does the rowing? Do you see the two knobs on the end of the dory? These knobs will keep the dory from bumping against the big sailing boat, when the men come back from fishing.

Fred begins to drop the fishing lines into the ocean. The long line is made heavy enough at one end so that it will sink down deep into the water. Fred fastens the other end of the line to one of the barrels which he brought from the boat. The barrel floats on the water and shows where his fishing line begins. Do you see the barrel?

Fred keeps dropping the fishing line into the water until the tub is empty. Then he takes another tub and puts that line into the water. He keeps on putting lines into the water until all his tubs are empty. Then the men go back to the big boat. They hope that they will catch a big fish on every hook.

Later in the day Fred and Joe row back. They keep rowing until they see one of their little barrels floating on the water. Then they begin to pull up the long line.

As the men pull the line in, they take the fish off

the hooks. They work fast, for the wind is cold. Water from the fish and line drips into the boat and on their clothes. Spray hits their faces now and then.

Soon they pull up a big codfish. As Joe lifts it out of the water, he calls to Fred to see how big it is. They put the fish to one side.

Then Joe pulls in another little line. It does not feel heavy, for the hook has nothing on it. Even the bait is gone. Joe knows that a fish ate the bait but did not get caught.

The men catch some fish which they do not want.

Some fish are not good to eat. Joe throws these fish back into the sea.

After the men have pulled in one long line, Fred rows the boat to another line. How can he tell where this line is? Then the men take the fish off this line. They go from line to line until they have pulled in all the lines which they put in the water. Their lines are put back into the tubs ready for the men to put bait on again. The dory is low in the water, for it has a heavy load of fish.

Then Joe and Fred row back to the big boat. They are proud of their boatload of fish.

When they reach the sailing boat, Joe and Fred must unload their dory first. They pile all their fish on a part of the deck which has been cleared. Some of the other men bring in their fish, too. Soon the deck is piled high with fish. The dories must be put back on deck.

As the men work, they talk about the fish which they have caught. Joe says it is the biggest pile of fish that he has ever brought in. The men will be busy all afternoon cleaning the fish and packing them in ice. Fred says that they ought to get a good price for such fine fish.

The captain comes out and looks over the fish. He looks all around at the ocean, for one dory has not yet come back. Soon the boat is seen. It gets back to the sailing boat. The fishermen tell how two of their lines had become tangled. It took a long time to get them fixed.

By this time the men are hungry. They can smell food cooking. They go inside the boat and take off their oilskins and boots. Then they wash up. There is a table in the room where they sleep. They sit down at the table and wait for the cook to bring their food.

See the men waiting for their dinner. Which is Fred? Which is Joe? What has the cook put on the table? Soon he brings out steaming food. He has made a good stew of meat and vegetables. He has fried slices of a big fish. The captain always sees that there is plenty of good food on his boat. He knows that the salt air will make his fishermen hungry.

Several of the men eat at the same time. Then they go back to work, and the other men come in and eat. The men often have fish to eat. Fred likes fish, but Joe does not. He says he likes to catch fish but never eats them.

The men eat fast, for they are hungry. Then they sit around the table and talk a little while before going back to work.

Do you see the bunks where the men sleep? What else do you see in this picture? Do the fishermen have much space to move around inside the boat?

All the time the boat is rocking on the waves. The fishermen do not notice the rocking. They feel at home on a boat.

After a while the men put on their oilskins and go on deck again.

See Fred and Joe at work. They each take a fish and cut it open. Next they clean the fish. Then they wash it in a tub of salt water. Where do you think they get the water?

The men must clean all the fish which they have caught. It takes them a long time. Fred and Joe do not talk as they work. They clean a fish and wash it. Then they reach for another. The other fishermen are also cleaning fish. The men work very fast, for all the fish of this catch must be cleaned quickly.

When Fred picks up a big fish, he holds it up for Joe to see. It is long and heavy. Joe says that such a big fish must be at least seven or eight years old or older.

After a while Joe looks out over the sea. There is not another boat in sight. All he can see is water and sky. Joe says the ocean is so big it always makes him feel very small. The sky is deep blue, and there are big white clouds floating along. The water goes up and down in waves. When the wind blows hard, Joe can see whitecaps here and there on the ocean.

As Joe and Fred clean the fish, they drop them

down into a part of the boat below them. Later in the afternoon Joe and Fred go below to pack the fish in ice. Then the fish will not spoil as long as they are covered with the ice.

See Joe picking up the fish with his long fork. Fred throws shovelfuls of chopped ice over the fish. Then the men put more fish on top of the ice and add more ice.

It is cold standing in the ice. The men have on their oilskins. Joe wears gloves to keep his hands warm. As they work, they can smell the fish. Their clothes smell of fish, too.

At last all of the fish are packed in ice below the deck of the boat. Before the fishermen can fish again, they must get their lines ready. They put bait on all the hooks again and coil the lines around inside a tub.

At night the men take turns watching the boat. If a storm is coming up, they must get the boat ready for it. The men fish several days in this way. They have a big load of fish. Then they put all the little dories back on deck and begin cleaning the last catch. The sailors pull up the sails and start home.

BRINGING IN THE FISH

The fishermen reach the town where they live. After the boat comes to the landing place, or wharf, they lower the sails. See the boat at the wharf.

Do you see Joe or Fred? Where do you think the dories are?

Now the fishermen have to unload the fish. How do you think they will do it? Do you see the little cart, or truck, standing on the wharf? It is just beyond the barrel. The men push this truck near the boat. Then they put the fish into it with big forks. When the truck is filled, one of the men pushes it along the wharf. You can see that the truck has wheels. The men must fill such trucks many times before they have unloaded all the fish. You can see how much work it takes to catch a big load of codfish and to unload them at the wharf.

As soon as the fish are unloaded, the captain tells the men when he will go to sea again. He

must sell the load of fish before the men can get their share of the money which the fish sell for.

Joe and Fred say good-bye to the other men and start home. Fred will soon see his wife and little girl. He has a fine big fish for his family. Joe will go to the hotel where he lives. The men are glad to get home again.

As they go along the streets, they smell fish. Many fishermen live in this town and bring their loads of fish here to sell. The whole town seems to smell like fish.

The fish in the trucks are taken to a building

near the wharf. At this building many workers get the fish ready to sell. They salt and dry some of the codfish and pack them in boxes. They freeze some of the fish so that they will keep. The place where this work is done is owned by a fish company. The company buys fish from many different fishermen.

In this picture you can see how the workers lay fish out in the sun to dry. Some of the dried fish are packed in wooden boxes and sold in our markets. Perhaps your butcher has cod to sell. Many large food markets sell fresh fish too.

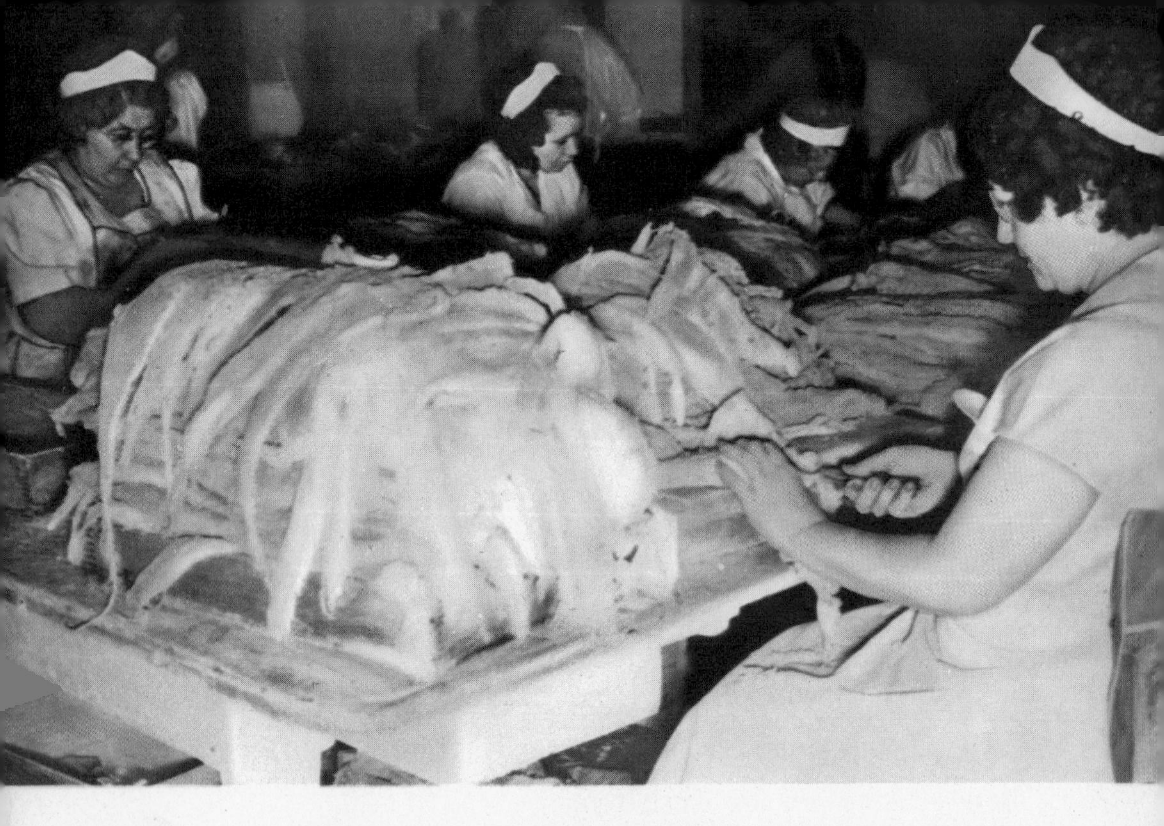

These women work for the fish company. They are taking bones out of the fish. They cut the fish off the bones in flat strips.

Not all cod are caught in the way which you have been reading about. Some fishermen do not use long lines with hooks. They do not go out on the ocean in little dories. They stay on a big boat and drag a big bag, or net, along the bottom of the ocean. The net gathers up the fish. Then the men draw it to the top of the water and pull it up on deck.

Would this way of fishing be easier for the men

than fishing with lines? Is it more dangerous to fish in a little dory or in a big boat? Why? In which way do you think the fishermen catch more fish? Why?

Sometimes the sky is gray and the air is wet out on the ocean. It may be so gray that the men can see only a little way ahead. We say that there is a fog. Have you ever been in a fog? The day may be clear when the fishermen start out in the dory. But before they can come back to the sailing boat, a fog may come up. Then it may be hard for them to find the boat. They may get lost on the big ocean. If a storm comes up, their little rowboat will be tossed about on the waves. It may even be overturned and the fishermen may lose their lives.

When it gets foggy, the sailing boat blows a horn that makes a loud noise. The men in the dories can hear the foghorn unless they are too far away. Sometimes they start back to the boat as soon as it gets foggy. But sometimes they stay to pull in their lines before they start back to the boat. Then they row as fast as they can toward the sound of the foghorn.

WHAT IS THE OCEAN?

Most of the world is ocean. All the land which you might see is only a small part of the world. The ocean has salt water. But rivers have fresh water. Almost all lakes have fresh water, too.

You can go out on the ocean so far that you cannot see land. Great ships may travel on the ocean for many days before they reach land.

Where the water is not very deep, we say it is shallow. There are many shallow places in the ocean. Usually it is shallow near the shore. But most of the ocean is deep.

The bottom of the ocean is smoother than the land in our country. The bottom has mountains, hills, and valleys, but they are not rough. In the deep sea it is quiet even though the top of the water is rough and stormy.

The ocean makes the land near it cooler in summer and warmer in winter. This is why people like to go to the beach in summer.

The Earth We Live On

OUR EARTH, A SPHERE

In this book you have read about the earth on which we live. The earth is very, very large. It is so large that many, many people live on it.

Our earth is round like a sphere, or globe. The earth is not quite a true sphere, for it is just a little flat at the poles.

No picture of our globe can show all of it. Half a sphere is called a hemisphere. Hemi means half. We live in the northern hemisphere. Do you know what northern means?

If at noon you turn your back to the sun, you will be facing toward the point on the earth called the north pole. East will be on your right and west on your left. South will be behind you.

In your next picture you will see the hemisphere that has the north pole as its center. The north pole is the point farthest north on our earth. North means toward the north pole.

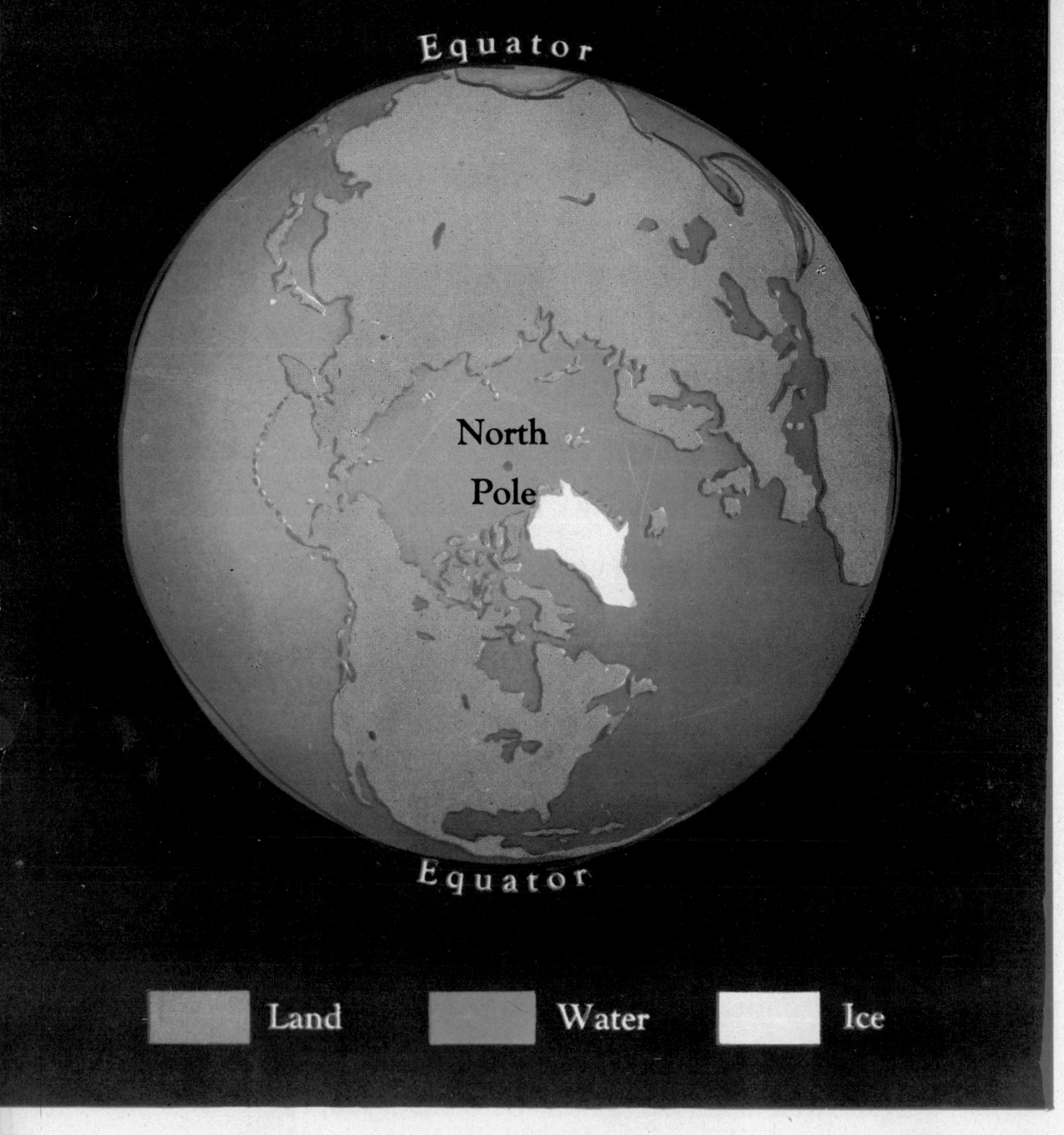

The ocean is colored blue in the picture. Lands that are covered with ice all the year round are white. Other land is brown. The north pole is in an ocean, but there is a ring of land almost all the

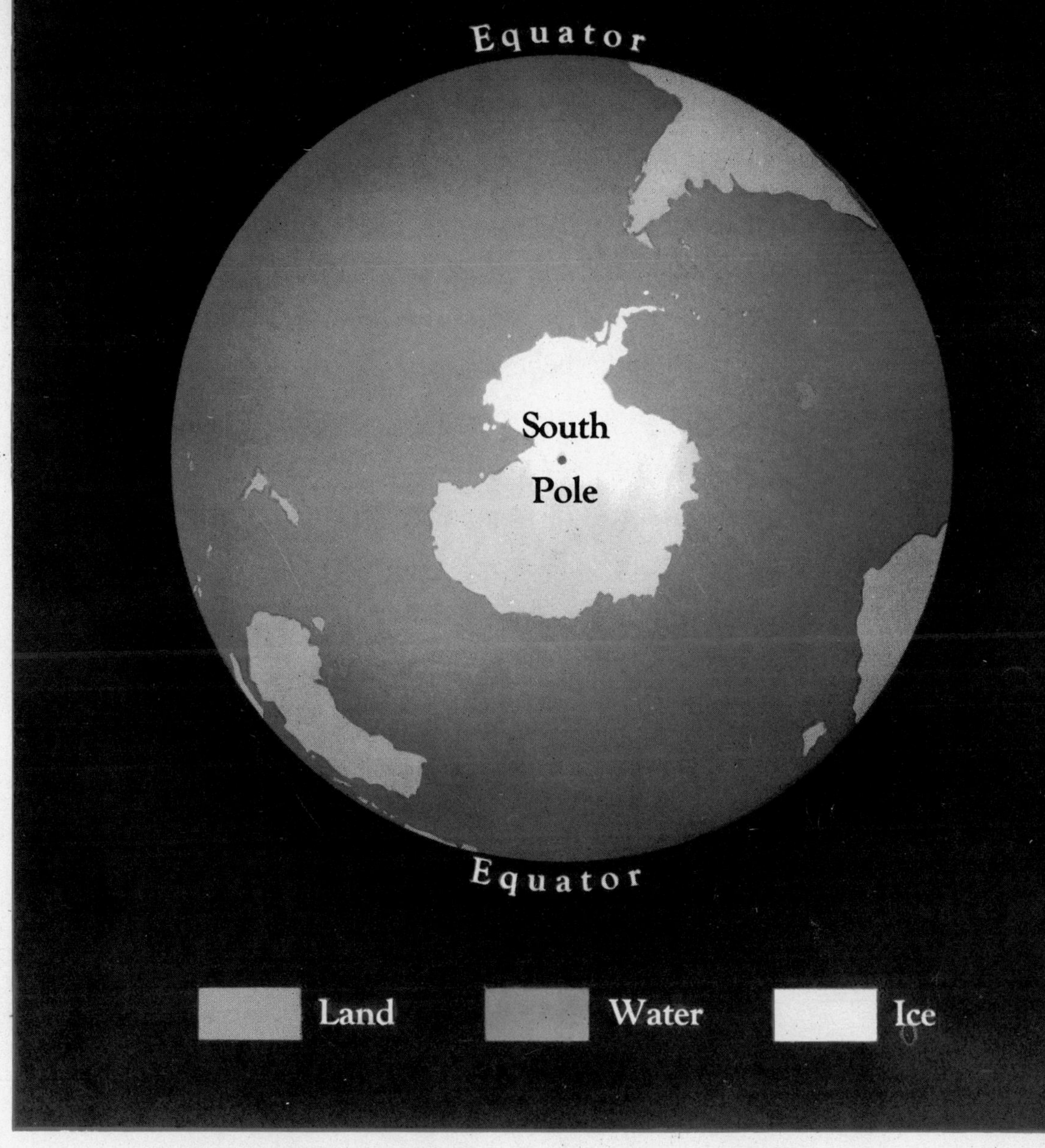

way around this ocean. Today men travel in airplanes quickly from the land on one side of the north pole to the land on the other side. Farthest south on the earth is the south pole. It is in the southern hemisphere. The south pole is on snow-covered land. A few islands are near this land, but beyond them there is water for a great distance.

Around the earth exactly halfway between the poles is a make-believe line called the equator. If you were to go to the equator, you would not see a real line. We say that a place is north or south of the equator. It is a long, long way from the equator to the poles.

On a clear night you can see a group of seven stars in the northern sky. This group of stars looks like a dipper with a long handle. The two stars which form the side of the dipper away from the handle point toward the North Star. When you face that star, you are facing north. If you were at the north pole, the North Star would be right over your head.

The stories in this book have told about the land and water on our part of the earth. Our world has nearly two and a half times as much water as land. So the land is really a small part of the whole earth. Much of the land is north of the equator. There is more than twice as much land north of the equator as south of it.

MOUNTAINS, HILLS, AND PLAINS

Where would you like to live, in the mountains, in the hills, or on a plain? Why? Most people live on plains or on the hilly land. Few people live in the mountains. It is hard to travel where the mountains are rocky and steep.

If you draw a picture of a mountain, you must make it smaller at the top than below. There are low mountains and high mountains. There are mountains with steep stony sides, and sometimes there are deep valleys between rocky ridges. The rivers in these valleys flow over big stones and make a lot of noise dashing on the rocks. Other mountains have rounded sides and shallow valleys where streams flow.

If you wanted to climb a hill or a low mountain, you might follow a trail that goes straight to the top. But if you wanted to climb a high mountain, the trail would start up a slanting slope and then turn and follow the slope in the other direction for a while. Always the trail goes higher and higher.

It takes many hours to climb a high mountain up a steep path. Some mountains are so high and rough and so hard to climb that only a few men have reached the top. There is one mountain which is so high that men have not yet been able to reach its top. When men try to climb a high mountain, they must take food for several days and maybe tents to sleep in. Sometimes snowstorms come up, and the men must camp until the storm is over. Wind may blow the snow about them, or fog may keep them from seeing how to go ahead. They may lose their way and get so cold that they cannot go on.

As you climb up a mountain, you see fewer large trees and more small ones. As you climb higher, perhaps you find only grass and weeds growing close to the ground. At the very top of the highest mountains, nothing grows. There are only rocks and snow on the top of high mountains.

Small trees can grow close to the ground on the windy tops of mountains. The wind is too strong for them to grow tall.

In summer many people like to go to the mountains to live. It is cooler there than on most level lands. Few people live in the high mountains all winter long unless their work makes them stay there.

A mountain peak is usually near other mountains. In our country there are places where high mountains stand in ranges. Some of these ranges go a long way across our country. The ranges are not straight but curve about in several directions. The mountain range in this picture is so far away that the mountains look blue.

If you were climbing in hilly land, you would not be very high above the rest of the land. You could not see distant hills. Hills are not high enough to be seen from as great a distance as mountains are. Hills are not high enough to have snow on them when the valleys below are green.

On level land you can often look ahead for a long way. In summer many of the level lands in our country are green. Wheat and corn and vegetables are raised on them. Here and there are houses where farmers live. There are big cities on level lands too.

FORESTS, FIELDS, AND DESERTS

You have read stories about forest lands where trees grow close together. Some forests are on level land, and some are on hilly land. Forests grow on the slopes of mountains too, if they are not very high. If the forest is on high land, the trees may be covered with snow in winter. If the wind does not shake the snow off, the branches may break.

In our country there is much level land on which people can farm. They plow the land and plant crops.

In some years there is enough rain to make the crops grow. In these years grass grows on the fields where it is wanted and where it is not wanted. Then dry years may come. The plowed soil is loose and blows away. Grass will not grow anywhere, not even in fields without crops.

On some land wild grass grows which makes

good pasture for sheep and cattle. There may be so much grass that the farmer does not have to feed his animals all the year round. But on many pastures it is too dry for trees to grow. Sheep and goats can find only a little to eat. This dry land should not be used for farming.

In mountain valleys wild grass often grows. This grass keeps the soil from washing away when rains fall. The water soaks into the ground and then runs off slowly. Small streams run down the mountain slopes and flow into larger streams. If the slopes of the valley were not covered with grass, the rain water would rush down the slope. It could wash away houses at the foot of the mountains. Then the people would need to build other houses in which to live.

There are desert lands in our country where few plants grow. Cattle grazing on these lands could not find much to eat. There is so little rain that the land is dry and bare. As you know, people do not live where they cannot get water. In some places there are stretches of sand where nothing grows.

LAKES, RIVERS, AND OCEANS

Do you live near a lake or a river or the ocean? Some lakes are little, and some are big. The water from a lake often flows into a river. The river may flow into another lake. Sometimes the river is wide, and sometimes it is narrow. It usually winds around and flows into another river, or it may flow a long distance all the way to the ocean.

Sometimes in mountains there are such hard rainstorms that the rivers are filled quickly. The water flows off the ground so fast that it washes away some of the soil. Trees near the riverbanks may be washed away. If grass and bushes grow along the bank, the stream cannot wash away the banks so fast.

You know that the ocean, or sea, is the largest body of water of all. If you look at the globe, you may think the earth is just one ocean with big islands in it. The largest islands in the world are

called continents. Between the continents are three big parts of the ocean, and each has a name. There are many smaller parts too.

The water in rivers and in nearly all lakes is fresh water. But the water in the ocean is salty.

On seacoasts the water rises and falls twice each day. This is called the tide. At high tide the waves may reach far up the beach. At low tide you must walk way out over the wet beach to reach the water. The tide is coming in or going out all the time. If you watch the waves along the beach, you can soon tell whether the tide is rising or falling.

THE CONTINENTS

You know the equator divides our earth into a northern hemisphere and a southern hemisphere. We live in the northern hemisphere.

There are other ways to divide our earth into hemispheres. Suppose you draw a line around the earth from the north pole to the south pole and then back to the north pole. If we draw these lines through the oceans, we say we have an eastern and a western hemisphere.

On the next page is a picture of the western hemisphere. It is made up mostly of two big continents and the ocean. The continent all of which is north of the equator is named North America. Our country, the United States, is part of this continent. The continent crossed by the equator is South America. Far south in the picture may be seen part of another continent called Antarctica. It is very cold in Antarctica. It is so cold that nobody lives there. The south pole is on this continent.

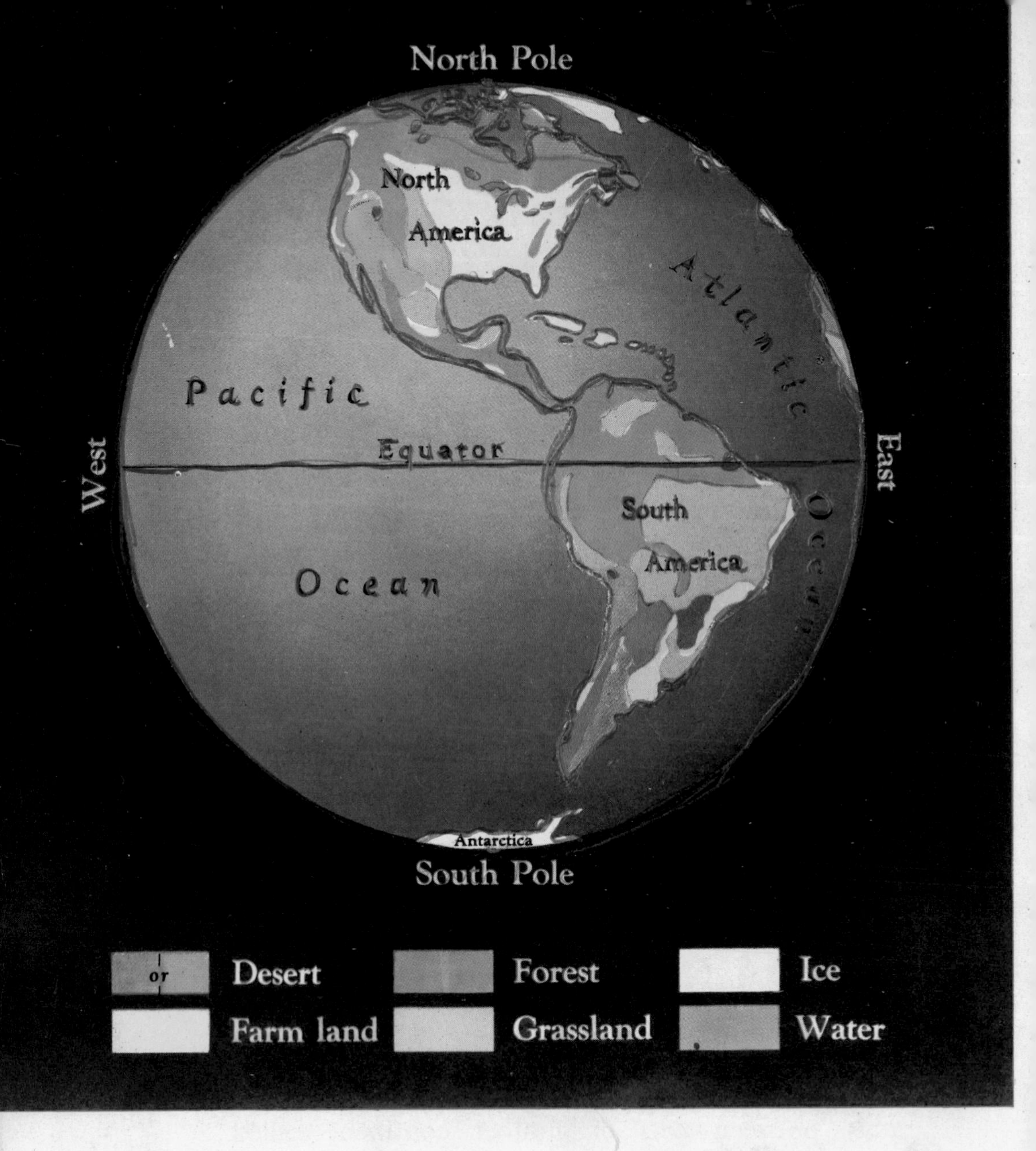

In this picture the land is not all of the same color. The key (blocks of color) at the bottom shows what kind of land is meant by each color.

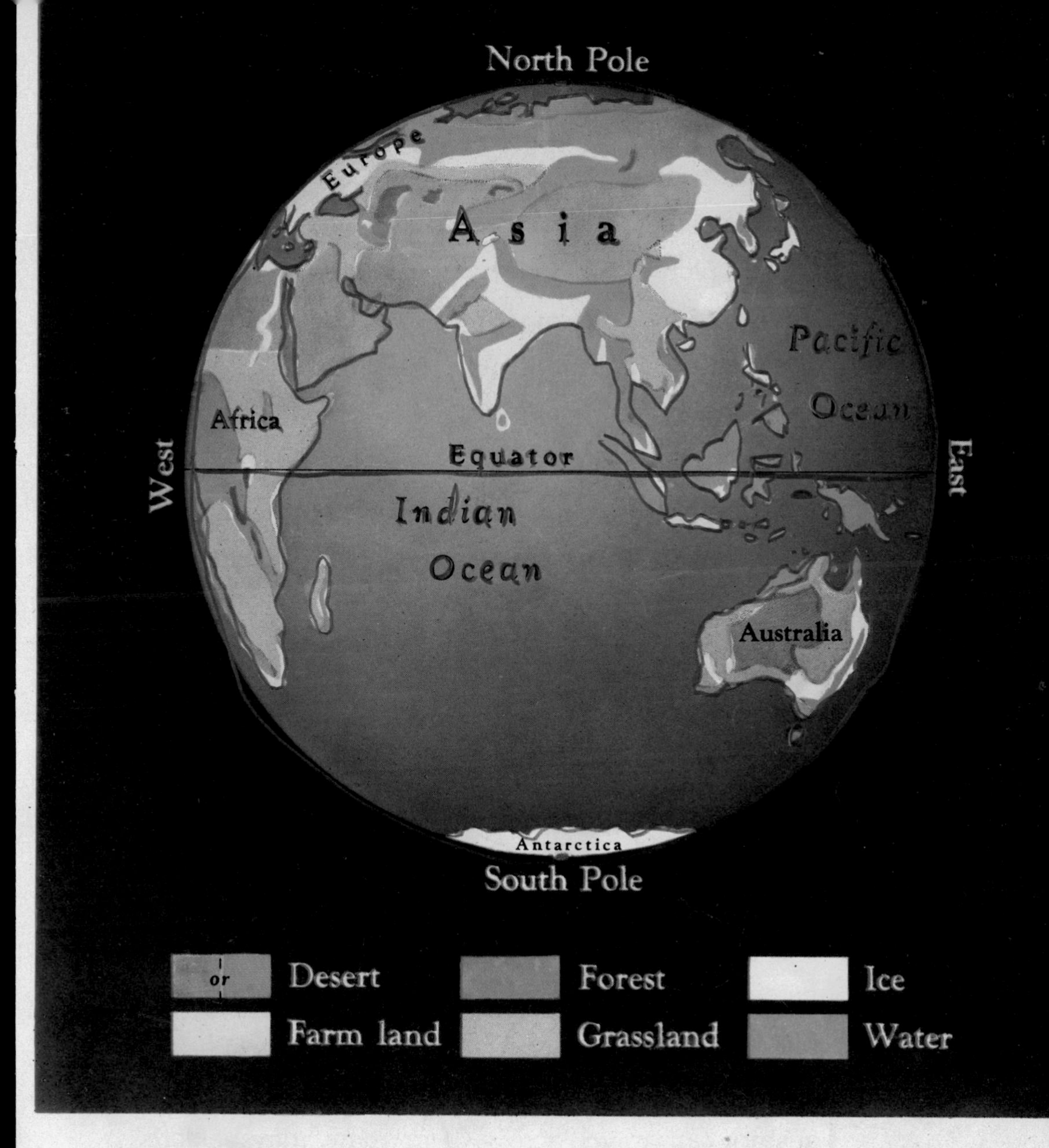

The green color means thick forests are on much of that part of the land. Antarctica is white because that land is cold and frozen. As in the other globes that have appeared in this book the water of the ocean is colored blue.

The picture on page 213 shows the eastern hemisphere. You can see four continents and part of Antarctica. Europe and Asia make up a big body of land. Sometimes these continents together are called Eurasia.

Africa is the larger of the two other continents in the eastern hemisphere. The big island of Australia is the smallest continent of all.

In the eastern hemisphere there are mountains, hills, and plains, just as in our own country. There are deserts, forests, and farm lands. There are lakes and rivers too. But this book has told about the land and water in our country only. Our country is only a small part of the whole world.

In the pictures showing the eastern and western hemispheres, you may see the names of three big parts of the ocean, the Atlantic, the Pacific, and the Indian Ocean. These oceans are so very large that a ship can travel across them many days before coming to land. Sailors use a compass to tell their directions as the ship travels from one continent to another.

Questions and Things to Do

About the Earth

1. What is the shape of our world, or the earth?

2. The earth looks flat to us because it is so very large that we can see only a tiny part of it at a time. Put your eye close to a big globe or a big round lamp shade. Does the part of it that you now see look round or flat?

3. On a globe point to the north pole and the south pole, and follow the equator around the earth.

4. What is a hemisphere?

Telling the Directions

1. What direction is north?

2. Point toward the north, the south, the east, the west.

3. When you face north, what direction is on your right? What direction is on your left?

4. The class may make four little signs for your schoolroom and put them up in the right places. On one sign write, "This way is north." What will you write on the others?

5. Ask someone to show you the Big Dipper and the North Star.

6. Tell why a ship needs a compass.

7. In what direction is the part of North America which is nearest the rising sun?

8. In what direction is the equator from the south pole?

About the Continents

1. What is a continent?

2. On which continent do we live? What is the name of our country?

3. Name two continents which lie mostly in the western hemisphere.

4. Name four continents which lie mostly in the eastern hemisphere.

5. Name one continent that lies almost equally in the two hemispheres.

6. Name the largest continent; name the smallest.

7. Name all continents crossed by the equator.

1. Is there more land or water on the face of the earth?

2. Tell what each of the following means: plain, valley, hill, mountain, canyon, mountain peak, range of mountains.

3. On what kind of land is it easiest to build a road?

4. Is it easy to build roads where you live?

5. If you have a sand table or an outdoor sand pile, make on it mountains, hills, level places, and streams. Remember that not all mountains are steep. Remember that streams always flow down. Remember that little streams flow into big streams. Make a steep path over a mountain. Make a road over a mountain. The road may go first one way and then the other, or zigzag, up the mountain.

6. Make a pencil drawing of a mountain range on a sheet of wrapping paper. Show some low mountains and some high ones, some with steep sides and others with rounded sides. On the high mountains show fewer and smaller trees near the top. What will you show at the very top of the highest mountains?

7. What kinds of work do men do in the mountains? What work is done in hilly lands? What work is done on plains?

8. How might a farmer use a field that is covered with grass?

9. What happens on slopes where men have cut down the trees and left no plants growing?

10. Make a list of things which you might see on a desert in our country.

11. What do we mean when we say seacoast? What is an island?

About the Water on the Earth

1. What does each of these words mean: lake, river, dam, ocean?

2. On a globe point out the large oceans. Remember that an ocean is bigger than the largest lake in the world. Remember that the largest ocean covers more of the earth than all the land covers.

3. Which is the larger, the Atlantic or the Pacific Ocean?

4. Ask your teacher to show you some lakes and rivers in the picture of the United States on your globe.

How We Get Food, Clothing, and Shelter

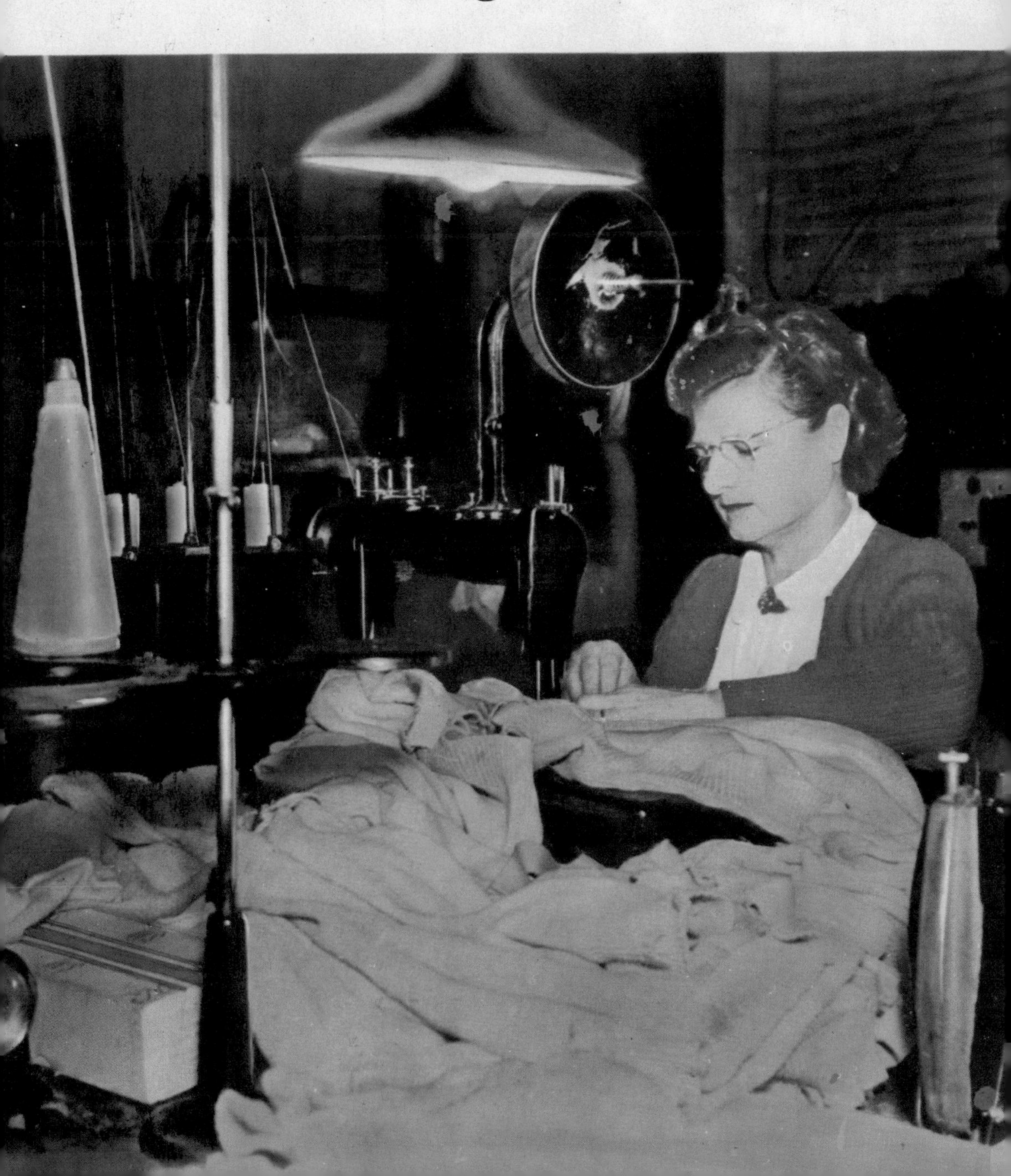

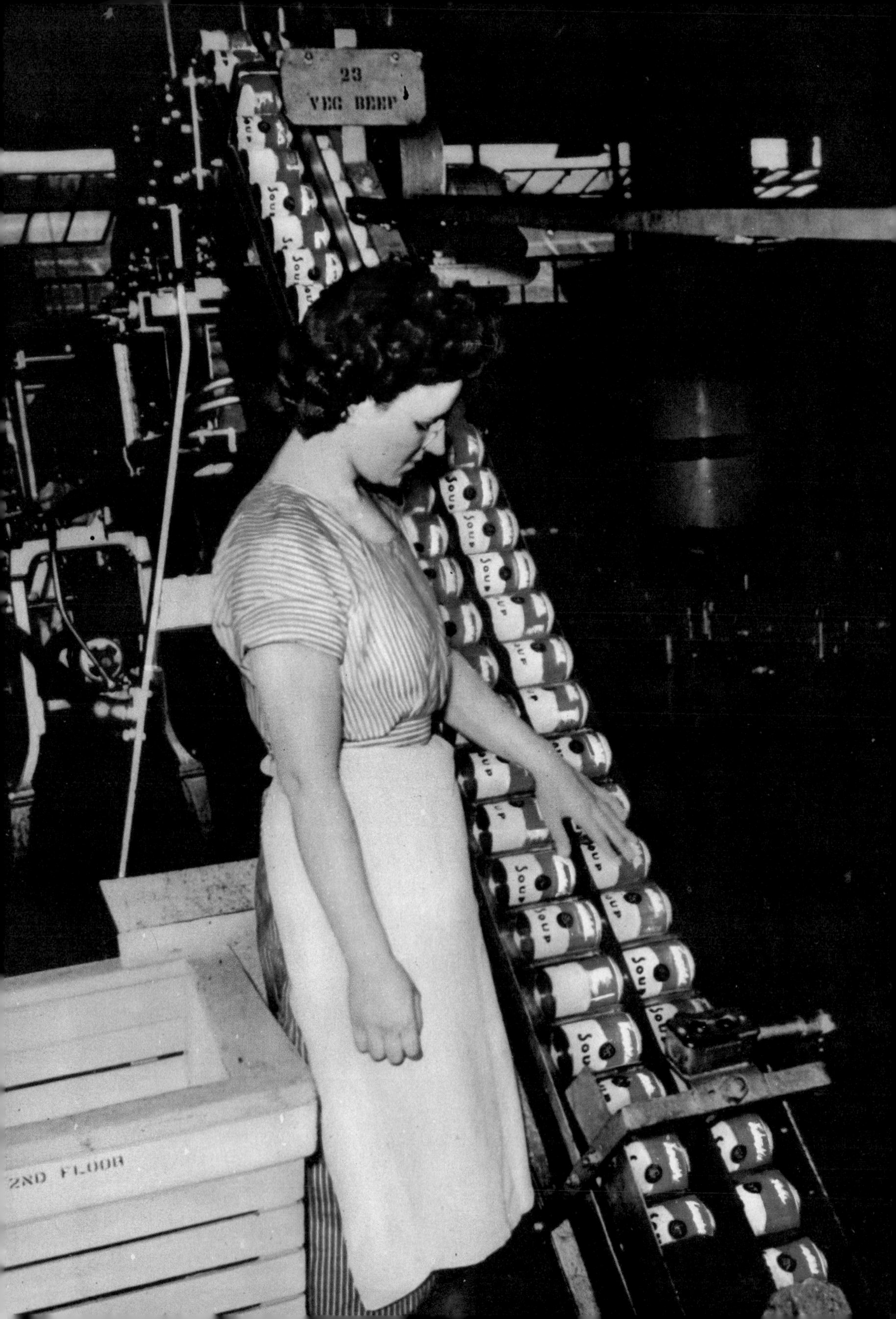
23
VEG BEEF
2ND FLOOR

WHAT EVERYBODY NEEDS

There are some things that we cannot get along without. Everybody has to have food to eat and water to drink. You could get along without playthings. But you could not live without food or water. Food is a necessity. Things that we cannot do without are called necessities.

For animals, too, food and drink are necessities. Animals eat plants. Some of them also eat the meat of other animals. When an animal cannot get the food that it needs, it soon dies.

Everybody has to have clothes to wear. In very cold weather you would quickly freeze if you did not have warm clothing. In hot weather you need clothes to protect you from the sun. Clothing, then, is also a necessity.

Even if you had plenty of food and clothing, you would need a place to sleep. You cannot live without some place to stay in away from the sun, wind, rain, snow, or cold. You need a house, or shelter. Shelter, then, is another necessity.

In our country men work day after day to get these necessities for themselves and their families. Farmers raise crops to sell to city people. Men and women in the city work in offices and factories. We say these people are making a living.

Men make their living in many different ways. In this book you have read about some of these ways. The herder takes care of his flock of sheep. The ranger cares for the forest. The fire fighter must always be ready to keep fires from spreading and burning down trees, houses, and other buildings. The farmer grows crops for food, raises animals for meat, and keeps cows for the milk they give. The lumberman cuts trees and sends the logs to the mill. The fisherman goes far out on the ocean to catch fish which are then sold in the market.

All these workers are making a living for themselves and their families. They are helping us to get food, clothing, and shelter. These are the three great necessities. Men get them from the earth.

HOW WE GET OUR FOOD AND DRINK

People eat many foods that come from plants. Some of these plants grow wild. Blackberry bushes grow wild in parts of our country. Most of our plant food comes, however, from plants that men grow for food.

Some stories in this book tell about how farmers grow corn. A great deal of corn is raised in our country.

In the summer people eat sweet corn. But you can get fresh corn for only a short time. Many farmers sell sweet corn to the canneries. There it is put into tin cans and cooked. It is good to eat when the can is opened.

Most of the corn that the farmers grow is not sweet corn but field corn. Farmers sell corn to factories that make it into breakfast food, sirup, meal, and many other things.

Field corn is fed to the animals that we raise for

food. Cattle eat corn. When pigs are turned loose in a cornfield, they eat much corn and grow fat.

You know, too, that the farmer uses some of his green corn and the cornstalks for silage. He keeps dried ears of corn for his pigs to eat in winter. These ears are kept in a corncrib.

There are many other food crops that our farmers raise. On many farms potatoes or tomatoes or beans or other vegetables are raised to sell.

Many farmers grow apples in their orchards. The trees stand in long straight rows. In other orchards peaches are grown. People need to eat plenty of vegetables and fruits.

In this book you have learned about maple sugar groves. Farmers get sap from these trees to make maple sugar and sirup.

Some of our food comes from animals. We kill wild animals such as rabbits for food, but we cannot get enough wild animals to go around. So farmers raise tame animals to give us meat.

They raise cattle and hogs. These animals eat the green grass and the corn that is grown for them. Most of the cattle in our country are raised where corn is grown. They grow fat and sleek.

Then they are taken to the city to be killed. They are skinned and cut up for the butcher to sell as meat.

Sheep, too, are sent to packing houses in the cities. The animals are killed quickly and every part is used. Do you remember reading about how sheep are raised on ranches and taken up into the mountains in the summer?

Some parts of hogs are made into sausage. Other parts are made into hams and bacon. The fat from hogs is made into lard.

There is a story in this book about a farmer's wife who raises chickens. Chickens and other tame birds that we use for food are called poultry. Almost every farmer raises chickens. You can nearly always buy chickens and eggs in the country.

Some farmers have large poultry farms. It is their business to keep hens to lay eggs to sell to other people. The farmer gets money for the eggs. Then he can buy the things he cannot make or grow.

The most necessary food in the world is the milk we drink. Very young babies cannot have any food but milk.

Do you remember about the farmer who took his milk to the cheese factory? Cheese is a very good food. But most farmers sell their milk to the people in cities.

These farmers raise cows on dairy farms within a day's journey of the city. In the summer the cows eat mostly grass. The farmer grows big fields of grass, which he cuts and dries for hay. This hay is food for his cows in wintertime. He also puts corn into his silo for winter feed.

Men catch different kinds of fish for food. They catch fish in lakes and streams. The ocean has such large numbers of fish that we can always get food from the ocean.

You have read some stories about a good kind of food fish, the cod. Many fishermen earn their living by catching cod in the Atlantic Ocean. They go far out to sea in boats and bring the fish to cities on the coast. Many cod are sold fresh. Many more are split open, salted, and dried.

In our country people get most of their food from crops raised on farms. Next to farming fishing is the way most often used to get food.

Water is very necessary to us. People cannot

live unless they can get water. In some parts of the world it rains a great deal. In those parts people have much more water than they need. In other parts of the world little rain falls. These parts are called deserts. People cannot live on a desert unless they can bring water to it.

Really all of our water comes from the ocean. Water is going out of the ocean into the air all the time. We say the air takes up the water. Then the air is damp. When the air has so much water that it cannot hold the water any longer, drops fall to the earth. We say that it rains. The rain sinks into the soil. It goes down into the earth. Sometimes we reach this water by digging a well.

Some of the rain water forms little streams that flow into big streams. Rivers flow on and on until they reach the ocean. They are really coming back to the ocean, for the water was there before the air drew it up.

We get most of our water from lakes and rivers. So you see that the food we eat comes from the land and the water, and the water we drink comes from the ocean.

HOW WE GET OUR CLOTHING

You have been learning how we get our food from plants and animals. Perhaps you never thought of it, but our clothes come from plants and animals just as our food does. A very few things, like the nails in our shoes, come from the ground instead. But almost everything we wear is made out of something from plants or animals.

In very cold parts of the world animals grow long, shaggy fur. This fur keeps them warm in the coldest weather. Men catch some of these animals in traps and kill them for their fur. They also raise such animals on farms for their fur. Many of the skins are used to make fur coats which people wear in the cold winter.

Most of our clothes are made out of cloth. Cloth is made of a great, great many fine threads. These threads run over and under other threads. They hold one another together to make cloth.

But what is thread made of? Woolen threads

are made of sheep's wool. These threads are used in sweaters and woolen underwear. They are made into cloth for warm suits, dresses, and overcoats.

Wool is cut from the sheep year after year and made into cloth. Sheep are raised in many parts of our country. You know how they are driven from pasture to pasture by sheep herders. They need a great deal of pasture land.

When the sheep's wool has grown long, men cut it off with machines. These machines are much like the clippers that a barber uses to cut your hair.

After the wool has been cut off, it is sent to factories. There it is made into cloth. Wool cloth is made in many woolen factories in our cities.

Not all thread is woolen thread. The kind that your mother uses to sew with is cotton thread. It is made of fibers, or threadlike parts, which come from seed pods of the cotton flower. The cotton plant is a bush, which grows from two to seven feet high.

Much cotton is raised in the southern part of our country. Some of the clothing our people wear is made of cotton. Not all cotton cloth is white. Some thread is dyed, or colored, before it is made into cloth. Some cloth is printed in several colors.

There is another kind of cloth that looks like cotton but is stronger and lasts longer. It is linen cloth made of linen thread. Linen thread is made from a plant called flax. In some parts of the world people grow a great deal of flax to make thread.

There is another kind of thread that has been very important to us but is not used so much now. This is silk, made of very fine fibers spun by the silkworm. We used to get much silk from other parts of the world.

Today we often use rayon instead of silk. Most rayon thread is made of fibers of wood which was ground up and softened in water. Rayon thread usually has a bright shine, or luster, just as silk has.

So you see two kinds of threads to make cloth come from animals. These are woolen and silk thread. Three other kinds come from plants. What kinds of thread are they?

Our shoes are made mostly from the skins of animals. In factories men take the hair off the skins. The skins are dried, made soft and smooth, and colored. Then the skin is called leather. It is ready to be made into shoes.

After thread has been made into cloth, the cloth must be made into garments for us to wear. After skins have been made into leather, men make the leather into shoes for us to buy. Most of this work is done in factories in our cities. Many people work in these factories to make the clothes that other people need.

Some of the things that we need last much longer than others. We use up food by eating it. We also wear out clothes. But if we are careful of our clothes, they will last for years.

HOW WE BUILD OUR HOUSES

The stories in this book have told you about some of the houses in our country. They have told you about the hut that the sheep herder lives in on the mountains. You remember reading about the farmhouse and how the farmer has space for his house and barn and sheds and a large yard. Also there was a log cabin in the woods where a family spent their vacation. Our country is so large that almost every kind of house is found somewhere.

Many of our houses are built of wood. Wood, or frame, houses are easier to build than stone houses. But if frame houses catch fire, they burn down easily.

In this book you have learned how we get wood from trees. Big trees are cut down, and the logs are sent to the mill. The round logs are sawed into flat boards which are made smooth by

machinery. Flat boards fit together better than round logs. It is easier to make walls and floors and roofs with them.

Where there are many big trees, it is easy to get boards, or lumber. But in deserts it is too dry for trees to grow. Many trees grow on mountain ranges in our country.

A wooden house is not so strong as one made of stone. Large buildings that are used by many people, such as churches and schools and stores, are often made of stone.

Sometimes stone is used for the walls of a building.

In some houses only the cellar walls are made of stone. The other walls may be made of wood or brick. Some stone is made very smooth and then used to make the inside of a building beautiful.

There are many houses with brick walls. Bricks are made out of clay. Clay is a smooth kind of earth that is found in many places all over the world. It becomes sticky when wet and can be easily pressed into the right shape. Then the bricks are baked in big ovens called kilns.

Bricks are of many different colors. You will see red bricks, yellow bricks, and white bricks.

Bricks could be used in almost any kind of building where stone could be used. Bricks are easy to put together. Men called bricklayers make walls of them. The bricklayers stick the bricks together with mortar. Mortar is made of sand, lime, and water. It is soft and sticky. When it dries, it is almost as hard as the bricks themselves.

In large cities houses often have many stories, one above another. City stores and factories often have many stories too. Tall buildings often have more than thirty stories. There is a row of windows for every story.

Any well-built house will keep us dry. But it will not keep us warm on a cold day. We need a fire to heat it.

Some people warm their houses by burning wood in stoves and fireplaces. On farms where there are patches of trees, farmers often cut down some of the trees to get fuel, or material for burning.

Coal is another fuel used in our country. You know what coal looks like. It is black and is in pieces ready to burn. It is found in layers in the earth, and men called miners dig it out. The coal is broken up into pieces of just the sizes that people want to buy. There are coal mines in many parts of our country.

People need fires not only to heat their houses, but also to cook with. In many cities people cook with natural gas. Such gas is found under the ground, or it may even come to the top of the ground. In other cities gas is made out of coal. This gas is kept in big tanks that are higher than people's homes. The gas flows through pipes under the streets to smaller pipes in the house. People sometimes heat their homes with gas. They may have a gas furnace or use gas heaters.

Questions and Things to Do

About Our Food

1. Why do we say that food is a necessity?

2. On the blackboard make a class list of plants that furnish us with food.

3. Why do we eat mostly food which comes from tame plants and tame animals?

4. In what ways do we eat corn?

5. Find out whether any breakfast food that you eat is made of corn. If it is, bring some of it to class and tell what you know about it.

6. Draw or copy a picture of an ear of corn without the husks. At the bottom of the picture write the word "corn."

7. What is a cannery?

8. Why do country people raise more fruits and vegetables than they can use themselves?

9. On the blackboard make a class list of animals whose meat you have eaten.

10. Tell what animal each of these kinds of meat comes from: pork, mutton, beef.

11. Here are the names of some foods. Put those that come from plants in one list. Put those that come from animals in another list. Roast beef, maple sugar, apple sauce, bread, butter, bacon, mutton, oatmeal, ice cream, codfish, cakes, eggs.

12. What do we mean when we say "poultry"?

13. What do we drink that comes from an animal?

14. If you live in the country and your father keeps cows, find out what he does to keep the milk cool and clean.

15. If you live in a city, find out what the milkman does to keep your milk cool and clean before he brings it to your home.

16. How are codfish caught? How are they kept from spoiling?

17. How do we get drinking water?

About Farming

1. What is meant by "harrowing a freshly plowed field"?

2. Make a class list of the farm machines that you have seen or read about. Tell what each

machine is used for and find a picture of each machine, perhaps in this book.

3. What might you see on a dairy farm?

4. Make a list of all the kinds of farm animals that you know about. Which are raised for meat? Which are raised for milk? Which are raised for eggs? Which are raised to do work? Which does the farmer's family keep for pets?

5. What farm buildings are used as shelters for animals?

6. If there are farms near your school, ask your teacher to take you for a visit to one. Find out what kind of farm it is. Is the ground level or hilly? What crops are grown? What farm animals are raised? What buildings are on the farm? Where does the farmer's water come from?

About Food for Animals

1. What is silage? What is a corncrib?

2. What plant food that farm animals eat do you often see growing wild?

3. What is hay?

4. Copy the names of the animals in the following list on a piece of paper and do not write in this book.

See whether you know what each animal eats. Write the names of its foods after the name of each animal, as:

Cows grass, corn, silage, hay, bran, cottonseed cake.

Pigs________________________________

Sheep_______________________________

Chickens____________________________

About Our Clothes

1. Make a class list of kinds of cloth and other materials that things you wear are made of.

2. There are several kinds of cloth. Where do we get the thread to make each kind of cloth?

3. You have read about cotton, woolen, silk, linen, and rayon cloth. Which of these kinds of cloth is often the thickest? Which is the smoothest? Which is the warmest? Which two kinds are the shiniest?

4. What is linen made of?

5. How do we use the long shaggy fur of animals in making coats?

6. Make a class list of things that are made of leather.

About Shelter

1. At home or in school make a birdhouse or a doghouse or a doll's house.

2. What is clay? What is mortar?

3. What things would you have to get along without if there were no more lumber?

4. If you can, watch bricklayers at work. See how the bricks are placed to make a wall strong.

5. Bring to school as many pictures of houses as you can find. Sort the pictures into three piles: frame houses, brick houses, and houses made mostly of stone. Ask your teacher whether these three groups of pictures may be put up in your room with the proper name above each group.

6. What is meant by the word "fuel"? Name all the kinds of fuel that you know of.

7. If your school is heated, find out what kind of fuel is used.

8. Tell what kind of fuel is used in your home for cooking.

9. Talk over what you would do if your home or your schoolhouse should catch fire.

10. In what season of the year is shelter most necessary?

INDEX

The part of this book which begins here is called an index. The index helps you to find the page or pages in the book which tell the story you may want to find. Look at the words in the index. All those beginning with *A* come first. Those beginning with *B* come next. Those beginning with *C* follow. With what letter do the next words begin?

After each word you will see one number or more numbers. These numbers tell the pages where you will find the story about that word. Sometimes there are two numbers with a line between them. Such numbers show the page on which the story of the word begins and the page where it ends.

Find the word *sheep* in the index. Is it near the beginning, the middle, or the end of the index? On what pages does this book tell about sheep? Find the word *cactus*. On which pages does the book tell about the cactus? Turn to these pages to see whether you are right.